THE REAL

PORN WARS

EXPLICIT CONTENT

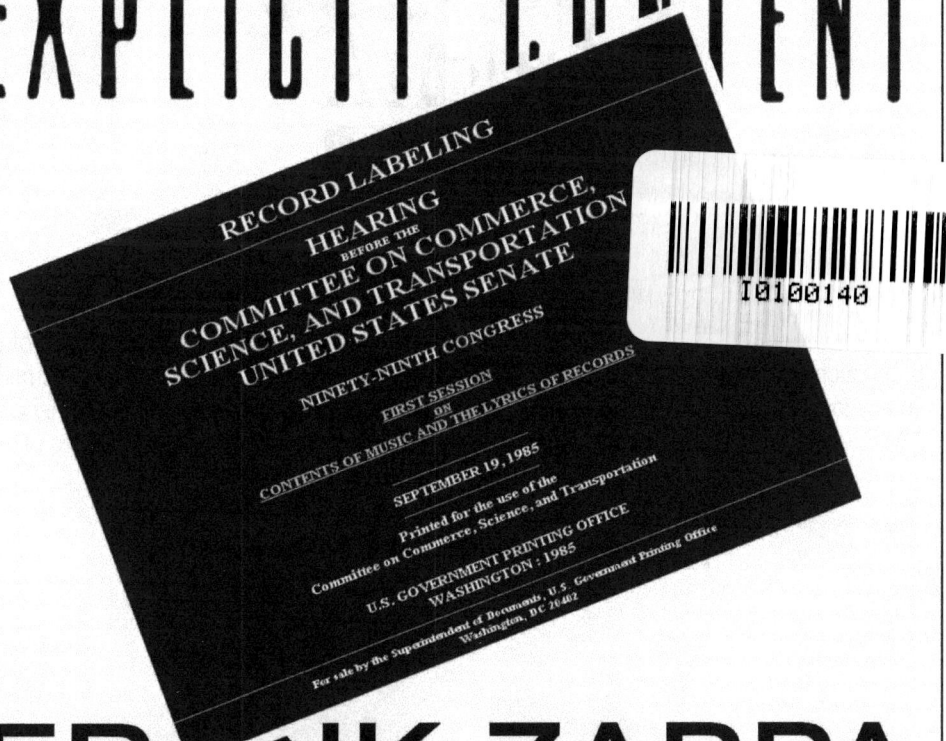

RECORD LABELING

HEARING
BEFORE THE
COMMITTEE ON COMMERCE,
SCIENCE, AND TRANSPORTATION
UNITED STATES SENATE

NINETY-NINTH CONGRESS

FIRST SESSION
ON

CONTENTS OF MUSIC AND THE LYRICS OF RECORDS

SEPTEMBER 19, 1985

Printed for the use of the
Committee on Commerce, Science, and Transportation

U.S. GOVERNMENT PRINTING OFFICE
WASHINGTON : 1985

For sale by the Superintendent of Documents, U.S. Government Printing Office
Washington, DC 20402

I0100140

FRANK ZAPPA

Edited by Clare-Elizabeth Bitakara'mire
Typeset by Jonathan Downes and Andrea Rider
Cover and Layout by SPiderKaT for CFZ Communications
Using Microsoft Word 2000, Microsoft Publisher 2000, Adobe Photoshop CS.

First published in Great Britain by Gonzo Multimedia

c/o Brooks City,
6th Floor New Baltic House
65 Fenchurch Street,
London EC3M 4BE
Fax: +44 (0)191 5121104
Tel: +44 (0) 191 5849144
International Numbers:
Germany: Freephone 08000 825 699
USA: Freephone 18666 747 289

© Gonzo Multimedia MMXIV

ISBN: 978-1-908728-44-9

Zappa wrote a "warning" which appeared on the inner sleeves of Frank Zappa Meets the Mothers of Prevention, which stated that the albums contained content "which a truly free society would neither fear nor suppress", and a "guarantee" which stated that the lyrics would not "cause eternal torment in the place where the guy with the horns and pointed stick conducts his business."

C O N T E N T S

LIST OF WITNESSES
Baker, Susan, Parents Music Resource Center ; accompanied by Pamela Howar,
president; Sally Nevius, treasurer; Tipper Gore; and Jeff Ling

Attachments
- Denver, John
- Fritts, Edward O., president, National Association of Broadcasters;
- William J. Steding, executive vice president, Central Broadcast Division, Bonneville International Corp.;
- Robert J. Sabatini, Jr., WRKC-FM, King College, Wilkes-Barre, PA;
- Cerphe Colwell, Reston, VA

Prepared statements:
- Mr. Fritts
- Mr. Steding
- Gortikov, Stanley M., president, Recording Industry Association of America, Inc.

Attachments
- Hawkins, Hon. Paula, U.S. Senator from Florida

Attachments
- Snider, Dee, of Twisted Sister

Attachments
- Stuessy, Dr. Joe, University of Texas at San Antonio, and Dr. Paul King, Memphis, TN

Prepared statement
- Waterman, Millie, National PTA vice president for legislative activity, Mentor, OH; accompanied by Arnold Fege, director, governmental relations
- Zappa, Frank, accompanied by Larry Stein, counsel

ADDITIONAL ARTICLES, LETTERS, AND STATEMENTS
- Bonk, James E., executive vice president, Camelot Enterprises, Inc., statement
- Bonniwell, Rev., R. Edgar, Faith Christian Fellowship Church: Letter
- Bradley, Hon. Tom, Mayor, city of Los Angeles, CA., statement
- Citizens Against Music Censorship, statement
- Gross, Martha Winter, Ph.D., statement
- Lynn, Barry W., legislative counsel, American Civil Liberties Union, letter
- Marmaduke, John H., president, Western Merchandisers, Hastings Books andRecords, statements
- MTV Networks Inc., statement
- National Radio Broadcasters Association, statement
- Radecki, Dr. Thomas. E, chairperson, National Coalition on Television Violence, statement
- Raucher, Glenn M., letter
- Stroud, Kandy, article
- Weiss, George David, president, Songwriters Guild of America, statement

I n common with many before the internet had been invented, Frank Zappa was an avid watcher of television, the medium by which everyone gained their knowledge of world (or at least American) events in those days. Early in 1985, by such means, he was alerted to the existence of the PMRC, which made no secret of its plans to censor popular music and, by extension, the people who created that music.

The PMRC was the Parents' Music Resource Center, and was started by Tipper Gore, the wife of Senator Al Gore, in response to what she saw as the filth peddled by a wide variety of recording artists. She claimed that America's children were in danger of being corrupted by rock music and that therefore she had a responsibility to do something about it. She and her friends, specifically wives of senators and businessmen, banded together as a pressure group with the stated aim of enabling parents to decide whether a particular piece of music was appropriate for their children to hear. As a non-profit group, the PMRC was not allowed to lobby for legislation to take place, so it was highly probable that some of the first people they pressured were their husbands. Who knows, they might even have used the old tried-and-tested device of withdrawing their sexual favours until the husbands agreed to attempt to turn the wives' self-righteous indignation into legislation.

As a lifelong advocate of free speech and expression, Frank saw the PMRC's stance as a threat to such freedom, and, as an interested party himself, namely a recording artist whose lyrics had often been misunderstood and indeed censored on occasion, he determined to do as much as he could to thwart the PMRC's sinister machinations. As an individual who knew his rights, he was aware that the proposal violated the First Amendment of the United States Constitution.

The PMRC's proposal was to have the recording industry regulate itself so that any lyric or piece of music it produced that was potentially offensive would have a warning sticker attached. It came up with a classification list of the different types of lyric subject matter that could conceivably offend people, such as V for songs that contained violent imagery, D/A for songs that advocated the use of drugs or alcohol, O for songs with an occult content and X for anything sexually explicit. It also compiled a list of fifteen songs they found offensive in various ways, mostly heavy rock or metal examples. It's worth remarking here that if it could only come up with fifteen songs then it wasn't doing its job very well – I can think of dozens which others could easily find offensive. However, satisfied that a point needed to be made, the PMRC then sent all of this information to the Recording Industry Association of America (RIAA), along with a letter demanding prompt action.

Realising who had signed the letter, namely a substantial number of Congressmens' wives, and just who comprised the PMRC, the president of the RIAA acceded immediately, and advised that certain artists' recording contracts would be examined, with the intention of seeing whether they could be altered to allow material to be censored. In August a number of major record companies announced that certain artists' records would be stickered with the words 'Parental Guidance: Explicit Lyrics'.

This wasn't good enough for the PMRC. The wives went into publicity mode, appearing on TV and radio, denouncing all sorts of songs, including Dancing In The Street, the old Martha Reeves & the Vandellas hit, lately re-recorded by David Bowie and Mick Jagger, camping it up for Live Aid. For myself, I have never had the slightest inkling of how this song could ever cause offence to anyone, given that it simply advocates having a good time while 'dancing in the street'. It doesn't indicate that dancing is simply the vertical expression of one's horizontal intentions, nor does it suggest that once in the street, ready for dancing, a person should take off their clothes before gyrating with wild abandon – it's just a simple, innocent suggestion to dance while not resident in a building, for the sheer fun of being alive enough to do so.

The PMRC claimed that there was a direct causal link between the type of rock music that offended people and all sorts of social ills, from crime to drug and alcohol abuse to sexual promiscuity, not that one piece of scientific experimental data was ever offered to support these findings. The mainstream press had a field day over what it called 'porn rock', but in response, the liberal press invited prominent rock musicians to comment.

Zappa decided to take on the PMRC as an individual rather than as a member of a counter pressure group and, as a result, spent a lot of his own money, sending out information packs and appearing on many TV and radio shows, sometimes in direct confrontation with a representative from the PMRC.

The PMRC's stance was that it likened the music industry to the film industry, which already had censorship, stickering, ratings and classification systems. Zappa pointed out time and again that the two industries could not be compared accurately, like for like. The film industry released about 300 films a year, while the record industry released about 25,000 songs. Who would possibly have the time to listen to all of these and decide whether to censor? What if one censor disagreed with another? Additionally, Frank drew the distinction between actors, who were 'hired to pretend' and musicians, who largely created their own material. If a film was adversely censored it would not have a detrimental effect on the actor, whereas a musician would suffer because he or she would be stigmatised as being synonymous with the type of material being censored. So, a song that mentioned an activity such as dancing in the street would have its performers labelled as lewd, dangerous and unacceptable.

It then transpired that many of the large chain stores that stocked mostly top forty material announced that they would not in future stock stickered albums, meaning that it would not be possible to do what I did as a child, which was to buy Motown Chartbusters Volume 3 in a high street record shop, because it contained – guess what? – Dancing In The Street by well-known menace to society Martha Reeves.

In September, under spousal pressure, Congressmen held a hearing, ostensibly to examine the state of 'porn rock' in the music industry, but in reality to try and recommend censorship as quickly as possible so that their wives would go away and leave them in peace to concentrate on investing in tax-avoidance schemes. To illustrate, Senator Hollings, whose wife was one of the signatories to the letter sent from the PMRC to the RIAA, announced that if he could do away with this sort of music constitutionally, he would.

The event that comprised the hearing in the Senate lasted only five hours, but was attended by a large number of interested parties from the media and was widely publicised. Personages from the world of popular music appeared in order to say their pieces, notably Dee Snider of Twisted Sister, who was able to disprove a number of the PMRC's claims, and John Denver, who was gently forthright in dismissing the PMRC's assertions, sticking to the point, made repeatedly, that there should not be any censorship whatsoever.

However, the most articulate spokesperson of the event was of course Frank Zappa. If I had been a member of the PMRC or one of their husbands I would not have wanted to have been on the receiving end of his devastating speech, which showed them to be the intellectual pygmies that they were, bland, ignorant and reactionary. Frank noted that country music had not been included in the proposals for censorship, and he pointed out that most of the songs written in the last forty years about sex, violence, alcohol and the devil were performed and written by country music practitioners, many of whom had spent time in jail for their activities. How was it that these ex-criminals, who waved the big flag of America, managed to sidestep the proposed moral censure?

Frank strongly objected to the wives' superior attitude, namely the idea that they knew better than anyone else just who should be censored and who should not. He observed that the subject matter that they wanted to censor was the same as that which fundamentalist Christians were most interested in doing away with. Sex, drugs, violence and the occult were matters abhorrent to the religious right, and Frank wondered if other fundamentalist obsessions, such as the pervasiveness of homosexuality, would one day be included in the list of matters offensive to the PMRC. For example, would the PMRC still allow music groups to exist but only as long as none of the singers were gay?

Regarding the issue of performers' recording contracts being re-examined, he made the point that groups and bands are comprised of individuals. If one member didn't toe the record company line about what was acceptable, did that mean that, as a result, all of the other members would suffer personally by being branded as associates of a person who was morally suspect? Spare a thought for the Vandellas, nowadays probably erstwhile friends of that ol' devil incarnate, Martha Reeves.

He concluded that the PMRC proposal was "an ill-conceived piece of nonsense which fails to deliver any real benefits to children, infringes the civil liberties of people who are not children, and promises to keep the courts busy for years dealing with the interpretation and enforcement problems inherent in the proposal's design".

So, what was the result of this intelligent and passionate objection to the activities of the PMRC and their senator husbands? Well, obviously, it being the United States, you wouldn't expect the concept of reason to be the uppermost principle on which were formed recommendations that would affect a large swathe of the population. Of course it's undeniable that citizens of the US have done great things, but on the other hand this is a country where bona fide psychopaths are legally allowed to own guns, for Christ's sake. With that sort of logic being prevalent in the minds of lawmakers, a seemingly insignificant issue such as censorship was never going to be given full and proper consideration and analysis. The fact that it concerns such trifles as the freedom of expression and the licence to create art, and the fact that these are two of the most desirable and necessary attitudes for a civilised society to promote, demonstrates to me that this country has its head up where the sun doesn't shine.

Accordingly, the PMRC's recommended action was put in place by the American music industry, and album cover labelling and stickering was introduced, although the aforementioned subject classification was dropped. Since that time, many musicians have criticised and parodied the situation. Indeed, many have made the point that an album cover sticker that advertised explicit lyric content would automatically attract a type of person already interested in sex and drugs and the devil, and in that regard it might be that the PMRC recommendations have been counterproductive to their purpose.

Frank himself parodied the cover labelling on his next album, Frank Zappa Meets The Mothers Of Prevention, released on his own label, Barking Pumpkin. The sleeve sported a Warning/Guarantee, which read as follows: 'This album contains material which a truly free society would neither fear nor suppress. In some socially retarded areas, religious fanatics and ultra-conservative political organisations violate your First Amendment Rights by attempting to censor rock and roll albums. We feel that this is unconstitutional and un-American. As an alternative to these government-supported programs (designed to keep you docile and ignorant), Barking Pumpkin is pleased to provide stimulating digital audio entertainment for those of you who have outgrown the ordinary. The language and concepts contained herein are guaranteed not to cause eternal torment in the place where the guy with the horns and pointed stick conducts his business. This guarantee is as real as the threats of the video fundamentalists who use attacks on rock music in their attempt to transform America into a nation of check-mailing nincompoops (in the name of Jesus Christ). If there is a hell, its fires wait for them, not us'.

The album's centrepiece track was Porn Wars, a sound collage piece containing music combined with fragments of speeches by the participants of the hearing. These have been treated electronically, slowed down, sped up and generally altered to make their utterances appear even more ridiculous than they already were. If you don't have the album already, I humbly suggest that it might be a good idea to buy it. It's a chance to listen to music that exists exactly as its creator meant it to be, without interference from the PMRC and RIAA.

At least Frank Zappa tried. He felt sufficiently strongly about people's right to free expression as to do as much as he could to combat those who sought to restrict that freedom. The following transcript of the Senate hearings of September 1985 demonstrate from the outset what he was up against.

Tim Scott
August 16th 2014

RECORD LABELING
THURSDAY, SEPTEMBER 19, 1985

U.S. Senate, Committee on Commerce, Science and Transportation, Washington, DC.
The Committee met, pursuant to notice, at 9:40 a.m., in room SR-253, Russell Senate Office Building, Hon. John Danforth (chairman of the committee) presiding.
Staff members assigned to this hearing: Kathy Meier, staff counsel; Dale Brown, professional staff member; and Cheryl Wallace, minority staff counsel.

OPENING STATEMENT BY THE CHAIRMAN

The CHAIRMAN. Ladies and gentlemen, this hearing is on the subject of the content of some, and I want to underscore the word "some," not all rock music, which it has been pointed out by a number of people as having really broken new ground as to the content of music and the lyrics that are used in music.

There have, I suppose, always been cases of songs that are suggestive in one way or another. However, certain rock music that is now being sold deals very explicitly with sexual subjects. Some music glorifies violence in various forms, sexual violence. Some music advocates the use of drugs, drug abuse, and so on.

And so, the reason for this hearing is not to promote any legislation. Indeed, I do not know of any suggestion that any legislation be passed. But to simply provide a forum for airing the issue itself, for ventilating the issue, for bringing it out into the public domain.

The concern is that the public at large should be aware of the existence of this kind of music, and the fact that it is now available to kids, and that kids of all ages are able to buy it.

It is my understanding that various private groups have been holding discussions with people who are in the music publishing and music industry to try to achieve some sort of understanding with respect to the labeling   of records so that at least the whole family knows what is in them, and not just the child who buys the record.

That seems to me to be a reasonable suggestion, but the point of this hearing is not for me to make any particular suggestions, but to simply provide forum so that the whole issue can be brought to the attention of the American people.

I want to say a word about this hearing. We have a number of witnesses. They have all been given specific time limits for their testimony, as is always the case in Commerce Committee hearings.

It is going to be necessary for me to enforce those time limits strictly, and therefore I would ask the witnesses to do so voluntarily.

Your prepared text of your statements will be included in the record automatically. You don't even have to ask for permission for them to be in the record. They will be included in the record automatically, so you don't have to take some of your time asking permission. It will be done.

With respect to the content of the statements, to describe what is in the music that is in question, will, I am sure, require some witnesses to use words and describe things that will shock the sensitivities of many of us in this room, and many who are watching these proceedings on television, and I just wanted to warn you of that in advance so that if children have the TV on, their parents can know what is in store for them.

I want witnesses to be able to inform the Senate of their points of view and the facts as they know them. But I would also hasten to say to witnesses that when you go beyond description and needlessly use expressions that may be in bad taste, this is a hearing of a Senate committee, and this is the Government of the people of this country. It is really theirs, and I would hope that standards would be used to the extent possible in your discussions and in your testimony which bears that in mind.
Senator Hollings.

OPENING STATEMENT BY SENATOR HOLLINGS

Senator HOLLINGS. Mr. Chairman, I first want to commend the Parents Music Resource Center for bringing this to the Nation's attention. I have had the opportunity to attend a showing, you might say, or presentation of this porn rock, as they call it. In the test of pornography, one of the things to look at is whether or not it has any redeeming social value. There could be an exception here, because having attended that presentation, the redeeming social value that I find is inaudible.

I have a hard time understanding it. Paul, since I traveled the country for 3 years, they said they could not understand me. Maybe I could make a good rock star. I do not know.

But in all candor , I would tell you it is outrageous filth, and we have got to do something about it. I take the tempered approach, of our distinguished chairman, and commend it. Yet, I would make the statement that if I could find some way constitutionally to do away with it, I would.

I noticed on the media yesterday morning something about a tax bill. I have looked into that. That does not pertain to this particular hearing, but we do know that the broadcast airwaves give more or less, the most limited of protected speech, because the airwaves do belong to the American public. They invade the privacy of the homes. We do know under the law of pornography that children are given a special protection.

I want everyone to know I am keeping that foremost in mind, and I am asking the best of constitutional minds, if there is some way in the world to try to limit it as we go along with the voluntary labeling . I commend those who are now beginning to label. That is what we would like to have, truth in labeling . I do not think we can outlaw pornography. I do not have that in mind at all. But take 6 to 7 hours daily – the average listening time, Senator, as I understand, by the youngsters of this particular porn rock and rock music and everything else of that kind. Well, let us say rock music and intersperse it with pornography. This is a matter of national concern, and it is something that we have got to give some kind of attention to within the constrictions of free speech.

So, I will be looking from the Senator's standpoint, not just to bring pressures to try to see if there is some constitutional provisions to tax, but an approach that can be used by the Congress to limit this outrageous filth, suggestive violence, suicide, and everything else in the Lord's world that you would not think of. Certainly the writers and framers of our first amendment never perhaps heard this music in their time, never considered the broadcast airwaves and certainly that being piped into people's homes willy nilly over the air. I will be listening closely.

I am sorry – we also have another Defense Appropriations mark-up – that I must leave here shortly, but I will be in and out. It is not because I am not interested. I am very interested in trying our level best to limit and control as best we can, for the tender young ears of America, the porn rock that will be presented here. I have heard some of it, and I am sure you have. The CHAIRMAN. Senator Trible.

OPENING STATEMENT BY SENATOR TRIBLE

Senator TRIBLE. Mr. Chairman, a brief statement if I may. More than 2,300 years ago Plato recognized that music is a powerful force in our lives, that music forms character and therefore plays an important part in determining social and political issues. In Plato's words, "When modes of music change, the fundamental laws of the state change with them."

Perhaps Daniel O'Connell, the 18th-century Irish nationalist, expressed it best when he said, "Let me write the songs of a nation, and I care not who makes its laws."

Our culture powerfully affects individual character. When we are constantly confronted by that which is coarse, we become coarsened. Repeated exposure to song lyrics describing rape, incest, sexual violence, and perversion is like sandpaper to the soul. It rubs raw one's sensibilities, resulting in a state of emotional numbness, in the words of George Will. One becomes literally demoralized.

Now, the subject [effects?] of suggestive [such?] lyrics on a [well-adjusted?] child may not be cataclysmic. Rather, the emotional damage is more subtle. The effect on a troubled child, however, can be disastrous, pushing that child over the emotional precipace , and to the extent that individual attitudes are influenced, this becomes a very real social problem.
The linkage between experience, thought, and action necessarily leads to concern about the consequences for society, and it demands a response from each of us, not the self-appointed guardians of the national morality, as someone suggested, but as concerned citizens and leaders of a great and lasting republic.

To paraphrase John Donne, any man's death or harm diminishes me because I am involved in mankind. Likewise, we are all involved in the American social and political experiment, and what damages our children and diminishes their future harms us all.

The mere announcement of this hearing led to cries of censorship. The issue before us, however, is not censorship. Censorship, according to the classic legal definition, is the review of publications for the purpose of prohibiting publication, distribution, or production of material deemed objectionable as obscene, indecent, or immoral. The key word in that definition is prohibition.

The issue before us is not prohibition, but rather the exercise of moral suasion, the labeling of offensive lyrics, and other efforts aimed at encouraging restraint regarding the time, place, and manner of certain speech in question. That does not constitute censorship.

The first amendment is not under attack here. The Constitution is many things to many people, but they do not serve it well, those who thoughtlessly invoke its words to defend their every word and action.

Mr. Chairman, I am a Senator, and I am also a father. Being a parent of two small children is the most important task I will ever have. If I were to serve in Congress for decades, and be acclaimed a great statesman, I will have failed in my life if I fail to serve my children's best interests, to protect them during their youth, and provide for their needs, to encourage their education.

These are all important, but I will be measured, indeed, we will all be measured by how we teach our children right from wrong, by whether we impart respect for self and for others, by whether we pass on to the future generations the sense of moral and ethical principle.

That is what this hearing is all about. I believe this may well be the most important hearing conducted by the Commerce Committee this year. I look forward to working with you and my colleagues on this committee, the Parents Music Resource Center , the recording and broadcast industries, and responsible citizens everywhere to respond to this very real problem. Thank you, Mr. Chariman.

The CHAIRMAN. Thank you, Senator Trible.

Senator Gore.

OPENING STATEMENT BY SENATOR GORE

Senator GORE. Thank you very much, Mr. Chairman. I would like to thank you and commend you for calling this hearing. Because my wife has been heavily involved in the evolution of this issue, I have gained quite a bit of familiarity with it, and I have really gained an education in what is involved.

The two most important things I have learned which have changed my initial attitude to this whole concern are, No. 1, the proposals made by those concerned about this problem do not involve a Government role of any kind whatsoever. They are not asking for any form of censorship or regulation of speech in any manner, shape, or form.

What they are asking for is whether or not the music industry can show some self-restraint and working together in a manner similar to that used by the movie industry, whether or not they can come up with a voluntary guide system for parents who wish to exercise what they believe to be their responsibilities to their children, to try to prevent their children from being exposed to material that is not appropriate for them.

The second thing I have learned over the past several months is that the kind of material in question is really very different from the kind of material which has caused similar controversies in past generations. It really is very different, and I think those who have not become familiar with this material will realize that fact when they see some of the examples that involve extremely popular groups that get an awful lot of play, some of the most popular groups around now.

I was interested when the hearing was first announced to have the opportunity to ask the heads of the record companies whether or not they felt some responsibility. I am told by staff that every single one of the chief executive officers invited to participate chose to decline that invitation.

I fully understand that, but I wanted to note that fact for the record, and I think that they should take a look at what their companies are doing and just ask themselves as human beings whether or not this is the way they want to spend their lives, if this is the way they want to earn a living, if this is the kind of contribution they want to make to the society in which we live.

No one is proposing or contemplating the government answering that question for them, but as citizens of this country it seems to me we have the right to ask them whether or not they wish to answer the question, and I hope that they will. Thank you, Mr. Chairman.

The CHAIRMAN. Senator Gore, thank you very much.

I want to point out that I have received a letter from Mr. Robert McConnell, vice president of CBS, stating that CBS received the invitation to appear here too late to prepare his testimony, that he is very interested in the hearings, and would be willing to appear at some later time. Senator Rockefeller.

Senator ROCKEFELLER. No statement, Mr. Chairman.

The CHAIRMAN. Senator Gorton.

Senator GORTON. Thank you, Mr. Chairman.

I am here to hear the witnesses, and I do not need to hold us off any further by any opening statement.

The CHAIRMAN. The first witness is Senator Paula Hawkins, who has joined us here at the committee dais. Senator Hawkins, we are delighted to have you here.

STATEMENT OF HON. PAULA HAWKINS, U.S. SENATOR FROM FLORIDA

Senator HAWKINS. I commend you, Mr. Chairman and the committee, for holding this all important hearing. As chairman of the Children, Family, Drugs, and Alcoholism Subcommittee, this is a subject that I am very familiar with.

The wealth of a nation is measured by its children. We decided as a committee in the last 18 months to hold hearings discussing the role of the media in drug abuse and prevention and education There we learned that by the fourth grade children have already decided whether or not to take drugs. We asked the question, does the media behave responsibly in portraying values to our children.

In the second hearing, on the issue of alcohol advertising in the broadcast media, we weighed heavily the first amendment considerations involved when the media portrayed behavior which many Americans find objectionable. Today we are raising the question how far should society go to keep young children from being exposed to images and words which may run counter to parents' values and beliefs and values.

It is the parent we blame if the child gets on drugs. It is the parent we blame if the child commits suicide. It is the parent we blame if the child burns down a building. Just how much guilt can we place on these parents without giving them some assistance?

As Senator Gore has so eloquently stated, it has been 30 years since Elvis first shook his hips on the Ed Sullivan Show, and here we are talking about the content of rock music and its presentation in records, on album covers, and advertising concerts, and in rock video. Much has changed since Elvis' seemingly innocent times. Subtleties, suggestions, and innuendo have given way to overt expressions and descriptions of often violent sexual acts, drug taking, and flirtations with the occult. The record album covers to me are self-explanatory.

I would like to show a sampling of record covers.

[The record covers follow]

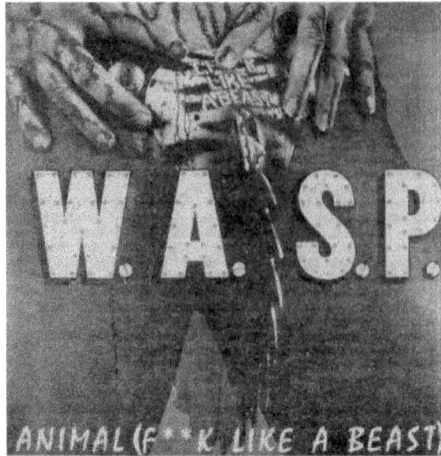

There is no question about the message. I still hear art is art, and in America artists are supposed to be free to express themselves, out who has the responsibility to regulate? Parents? The music industry? The Government?

I speak as a legislator. I speak as a parent, a veteran who has brought three children through adolescence. I know the temptations dangled in front of teenagers and I know the frustrations parents experience all through this process. The sense of hopelessness when you get the feeling your child will not listen to you.

There is in these times often a need to look to a force outside yourself for help. The question we must ask is, should the force be the Government, and that is what this hearing is designed to determine.

I believe it will be helpful before we proceed any further to get an idea of what it is we are talking about.

One criticism of the rock industry is the way it portrays values in rock videos which are viewed by the kids. There are suggestions that the move to label rock albums be extended to videos as well. I do not watch much television. I am not sure how many of my colleagues get much opportunity to watch any of the music video shows now available on cable and free TV. I brought along two videos from which to choose which I believe are representative of the kind of presentations which cause the problem. The first is by the group *Van Halen.*

[The rock video Hot for Teacher by *Van Halen* was shown.]

The CHAIRMAN. Senator Hawkins, just a minute.

Now, this is a very large crowd today. We have allowed people in beyond the capacity of this room. We are not going to have any demonstrations. No applause, no demonstrations of any kind.

Senator HAWKINS. I thank the chairman. The title of that tape was "Hot for Teacher."

The next video is by the group Twisted Sister, and we will show you a brief portion of that. This is a very popular video.

[The video We're Not Going to Take It by *Twisted Sister* was shown.]

Senator HAWKINS. Mr. Chairman, I think a picture is worth a thousand words. This issue is too hot not to cool down. Parents are asking for assistance, and I hope we always remember that no success in life would compensate for failure in the home.

The CHAIRMAN. Senator Hawkins, thank you very much.

The next witness is Susan Baker, Mrs. James Baker, from the Parents Music Resource Center. Mrs. Baker, thank you very much for being with us. Please proceed.

STATEMENT OF SUSAN BAKER, PARENTS MUSIC RESOURCE CENTER, ACCOMPANIED BY PAMELA HOWAR, PRESIDENT; SALLY NEVIUS, TREASURER; TIPPER GORE; AND JEFF LING

Mrs. BAKER. Thank you very much, Mr. Chairman. We would like to thank you and the committee for the opportunity to testify before you.

The CHAIRMAN. Could you please speak directly into the microphone, thank you.

Mrs. BAKER. Before I begin, I would like to introduce the president of the PMRC, Pam Howar, and our treasurer, Sally Nevius.

The Parents Music Resource Center   was organized in May of this year by mothers of young children who are very concerned by the growing trend in music toward lyrics that are sexually explicit, excessively violent, or glorify the use of drugs and alcohol.

Our primary purpose is to educate and inform parents about this alarming trend as well as to ask the industry to exercise self-restraint.

It is no secret that today's rock music is a very important part of adolescence and teenagers' lives. It always has been, and we don't question their right to have their own music. We think that is important. They use it to identify and give expression to their feelings, their problems, their joys, sorrows, loves, and values. It wakes them up in the morning and it is in the background as they get dressed for school. It is played on the bus. It is listened to in the cafeteria during lunch. It is played as they do their homework. They even watch it on MTV now. It is danced to at parties, and puts them to sleep at night.

Because anything that we are exposed to that much has some influence on us, we believe that the music industry has a special responsibility as the message of songs goes from the suggestive to the blatantly explicit.

As Ellen Goodman stated in a recent column, rock ratings:

The outrageous edge of rock and roll has shifted its focus from Elvis's pelvis to the saw protruding from Blackie Lawless's codpiece on a *WASP* album. Rock lyrics have turned from "I can't get no satisfaction" to "I am going to force you at gunpoint to eat me alive."

The material we are concerned about cannot be compared with Louie Louie, Cole Porter, Billie Holliday, et cetera. Cole Porter's "the birds do it, the bees do it," can hardly be compared with WASP, "I f-u-c-k like a beast." There is a new element of vulgarity and violence toward women that is unprecedented.

While a few outrageous recordings have always existed in the past, the proliferation of songs glorifying rape, sadomasochism, incest, the occult, and suicide by a growing number of bands illustrates this escalating trend that is alarming.

Some have suggested that the records in question are only a minute element in this music. However, these records are not few, and have sold millions of copies, like Prince's "Darling Nikki," about masturbation, sold over 10 million copies. *Judas Priest*, the one about forced oral sex at gunpoint, has sold over 2 million copies. *Quiet Riot*, "Metal Health," has songs about explicit sex, over 5 million copies. *Motley Crue*, "Shout at the Devil," which contains violence and brutality to women, over 2 million copies.

Some say there is no cause for concern. We believe there is. Teen pregnancies and teenage suicide rates are at epidemic proportions today. The Noedecker Report states that in the United States of America we have the highest teen pregnancy rate of any developed country: 96 out of 1,000 teenage girls become pregnant.

Rape is up 7 percent in the latest statistics, and the suicide rates of youth between 16 and 24 has gone up 300 percent in the last three decades while the adult level has remained the same. There certainly are many causes for these ills in our society, but it is our contention that the pervasive messages aimed at children which promote and glorify suicide, rape, sadomasochism, and so on, have to be numbered among the contributing factors.

Some rock artists actually seem to encourage teen suicide. Ozzie Osbourne sings "Suicide Solution." *Blue Oyster Cult* sings "Don't Fear the Reaper." *AC/DC* sings "Shoot to Thrill." Just last week in Centerpoint, a small Texas town, a young man took his life while listening to the music of *AC/DC*. He was not the first.

Now that more and more elementary school children are becoming consumers of rock music, we think it is imperative to discuss this question. What can be done to help parents who want to protect their children from these messages if they want to?

Today parents have no way of knowing the content of music products that their children are buying. While some album covers are sexually explicit or depict violence, many others give no clue as to the content. One of the top 10 today is *Morris Day and the Time*, "Jungle Love." If you go to buy the album "Ice Cream Castles" to get "Jungle Love," you also get, "If the Kid Can't Make You Come, Nobody Can," a sexually explicit song.

The pleasant cover picture of the members of the band gives no hint that it contains material that is not appropriate for young consumers.

Our children are faced with so many choices today. What is available to them through the media is historically unique. The Robert Johnson study on teen environment states that young people themselves often feel that they have: one, too many choices to make: two, too few structured means for arriving at decisions: and three, too little help to get there.

We believe something can be done, and Tipper Gore will discuss the possible solution. Thank you.

Mrs. GORE. Thank you, Mr. Chairman.

We are asking the recording industry to voluntarily assist parents who are concerned by placing a warning label on music products inappropriate for younger children due to explicit sexual or violent lyrics.

The Parents Music Resource Center   originally proposed a categorical rating system for explicit material. After many discussions with the record industry, we recognize some of the logistical and economic problems, and have adjusted our original suggestions accordingly. We now propose one generic warning label to inform consumers in the marketplace about lyric content. The labels would apply to all music.

We have asked the record companies to voluntarily label their own products and assume responsibility for making those judgments. We ask the record industry to appoint a one-time panel to recommend a uniform set of criteria which could serve as a policy guide for the individual companies. Those individual recording companies would then in good faith agree to adhere to this standard, and make decisions internally about which records should be labeled according to the industry criteria.

We have also asked that lyrics for labeled   music products be available to the consumer before purchase in the marketplace. Now, it is important to clearly state what our proposal is not.

A voluntary labeling is not censorship. Censorship implies restricting access or suppressing content. This proposal does neither. Moreover, it involves no Government action. Voluntary labeling in no way infringes upon first amendment rights. Labeling is little more than truth in packaging, by now, a time honored principle in our free enterprise system, and without labeling , parental guidance is virtually impossible.

Most importantly, the committee should understand the Parents Music Resource Center is not advocating any Federal intervention or legislation whatsoever. The excesses that we are discussing were allowed to develop in the marketplace, and we believe the solutions to these excesses should come from the industry who has allowed them to develop and not from the Government.

The issue here is larger than violent and sexually explicit lyrics. It is one of ideas and ideal freedoms and responsibility in our society. Clearly, there is a tension here, and in a free society there always will be. We are simply asking that these corporate and artistic rights be exercised with responsibility, with sensitivity, and some measure of self-restraint, especially since young minds are at stake. We are talking about preteenagers and young teenagers having access to this material. That is our point of departure and our concern.

Now, Mr. Chairman, one point we have already made, that the material that has caused the concern is new and different. It is not just a continuation of controversies of past generations. To illustrate this point, we would like to show a slide presentation, and to this end I turn the microphone over to Jeff Ling, who is a consultant to our group, and he will show you some of the material that we are talking about.

Thank you.

Mr. LING. Mr. Chairman, if we could have the lights turned down.

[Slides were then shown.]

Mr. LING. Mr. Chairman and distinguished members of the committee, thank you for allowing me to speak to you today. The purpose of this presentation is to acquaint you with the type of material that is in question.

I will be covering the themes of violence and sexuality. Bear in mind that what you are about to see and hear is a small sample of the abundant material available today. Today the element of violent, brutal erotica has exploded in rock music in an unprecedented way. Many albums today include songs that encourage suicide, violent revenge, sexual violence, and violence just for violence's sake.

This is Steve Boucher. Steve died while listening to *AC/DC's* "Shoot to Thrill." Steve fired his father's gun into his mouth.

[Editor's note: we could not source a picture of this boy]

A few days ago I was speaking in San Antonio. The day before I arrived, they buried a young high school student. This young man had taken his tape deck to the football field.

He hung himself while listening to *AC/DC's* "Shoot to Thrill." Suicide has become epidemic in our country among teenagers.

Some 6,000 will take their lives this year. Many of these young people find encouragement from some rock stars who present death as a positive, almost attractive alternative.

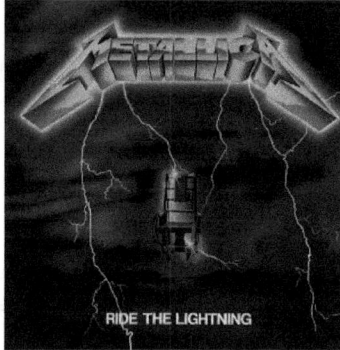

The album I am holding up in front of you is by the band Metallica . It is on Electra Asylum records. A song on this album is called "Faith in Black" [Fade to Black]. It says the following. "I have lost the will to live. Simply nothing more to give. There is nothing more for me. I need the end to set me free."

"Death greets me warm. I will just say good-bye."

Consider the self-destructive violence that is encouraged in their song "Whiplash." "Bang your head against the stage like you never have before. Make it rain, make it bleed, make it really sore. In a frenzied madness, now is the time to let it rip, to let it fucking loose. We are gathered here to maim and kill, for this is what we choose."

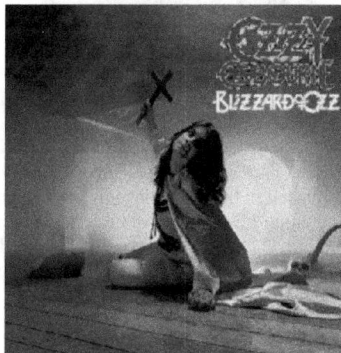

Ozzie Osbourne [sic] on his first solo album, shown here, sings a song called "Suicide

Solution." [*] Ozzie insists that he in no way encourages suicidal behavior in young people, and yet he appears in photographs such as these in periodicals that are geared toward the young teenage audience.

For those of you who cannot make that out because of the lights, it is a picture of Ozzie with a gun barrel stuck into his mouth. [EDITOR'S NOTE: We couldn't find the picture alluded to, but we did find the picture above that carries much the same message]

This is the cover of *Twisted Sister's* high selling LP for Atlantic Records called "Stay Hungry." An example of Twisted Sister's appeal to young people is evident in the back to school contest being run by MTV. First prize is a get together with *Twisted Sister*. The first prize is a meeting with *Twisted Sister*.

* The song "Suicide Solution" has met with its share of controversy, most notably the October 1984 suicide of John McCollum, a depressed teenager who shot himself in the head allegedly after listening to the song. The boy's parents sued Osbourne and CBS Records for "encouraging self-destructive behavior" in young persons who were "especially susceptible" to dangerous influences (McCollum et al. v. CBS, Inc., et al.). In his defence, Osbourne stated in court that when the song was being written the words "Wine is fine but whiskey's quicker..." came to him suddenly and were a reflection not on the merits of suicide but rather on the death of AC/DC vocalist Bon Scott, a friend of Osbourne's who had recently died of alcohol-related misadventure. Bob Daisley, who wrote the majority of the song's lyrics, has stated that he actually had Osbourne's own substance abuse issues in mind when he composed the song. The McCollums' complaint was dismissed on the grounds that the First Amendment protected Osbourne's right to free artistic expression. (Wikipedia)

The hit song from the album, "We're Not Going to Take It," was released as a video, which you saw just a moment ago, a video in which the band members proceed to beat up daddy, who will not let them rock. Their first album, which has been rereleased by Atlantic Records, is called "Under the Blade."

The title song includes words like "Your hands are tied, your legs are strapped, you are going under the blade." In lyrics from the song "Shoot them Down," the band sings, "They think we are fools who want to make their own rules. It only gets us madder. They think they are hot. Well, I say they're not. They shoot us down for fun. If they don't want to play, then let's make them pay. Shoot them down with a fucking gun."

This is the cover of *AC/DC's* brand new album for Atlantic Records, "Fly on the Wall."

One of the songs from the album "Back in Business" was released as a single for airplay and included the words, "Don't you struggle or try to bite. You want some trouble. I am the king of vice. I am a wrecking ball. I am a stinging knife. Steal your money. Going to take your life." Of course, *AC/DC* is no stranger to violent material. Their song "Squealer" contained the following. "She said she had never been balled before, and I don't think she'll ball no more. Fixed her good."

One of their fans I know you are aware of is the accused *Night Stalker*.

Judas Priest sings of violent rape in their song "Eat Me Alive" from their Columbia Records released "Defenders of the Faith." "Squealing in passion as the rod of steel injects. Gut wrenching frenzy that deranges every joint. I am going to force you at gunpoint to eat me alive."

The band *Great White* in their album "On Their Knees" sings these words "Knocking down your door, going to pull you to the floor, taking what I choose, never going to lose, going to drive my love inside you, going to nail your ass to the floor."

This is *Motley Crue*. Their albums for Electra Asylum sell millions, and they are one of the top 10 grossing concert bands this year. Their albums include songs like "Bastard." "Out goes the light. In goes my knife. Pull out his life. Consider that bastard dead."

"Live Wire." "I will either break her face or take down her legs. Get my ways at will. Go for the throat and never let loose. Going in for the kill."

And "Too Young to Fall in Love." "Not a woman, but a whore. I can taste the hate. Well, now I am killing you. Watch your face turning blue."

This is the cover of the new album by the band *Abattoir*.

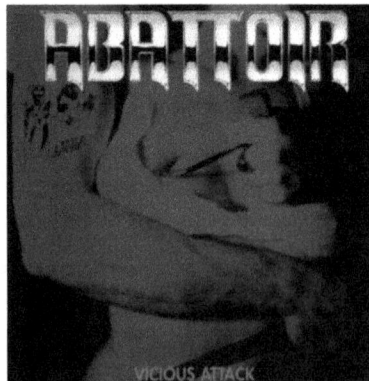

The title song is about a homicidal maniac, and notice on the cover the arms of the man wrapped around the woman. In one hand is a long knife. The other hand holds a hook being pressed against the woman's breast.

This is the cover of an album entitled "Rise of the Mutants" by the band *Impaler*.

Notice the man with the bloody meat in his mouth and hand. He is kneeling over the bloody arm of a woman.

The back cover shows a woman with a bloody face at the feet of the drummer.

While both of these albums were released on independent labels as opposed to major labels, they are reviewed and featured in teen rock magazines and are available in local record stores.

This band, *WASP*, recently signed a $1.5 million contract with Capital Records. This is their first release. The capital item is entitled "The Torture Never Stops." Violence permeates the album as well as their stage show, which has included chopping up and throwing raw meat into the audience.

Drinking blood from a skull.

And until recently the simulated rape and murder of a half-nude woman.

This single is available in record stores across the country. The cover features the cod piece that lead singer Blackie Lawless wears on stage. In this picture, there is blood dripping down his stomach, hands, and off of the blade between his legs. The song that accompanies this photo is "Fuck Like a Beast."

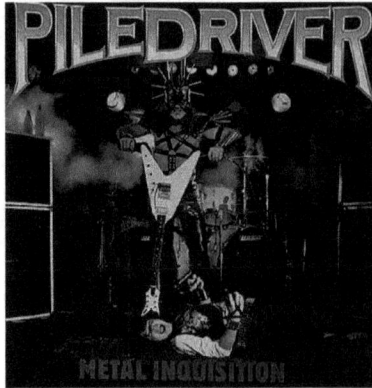

This band, *Piledriver*, fuses together the elements of sexual violence and occult in the song "Lust." I forgot. It is right here in front of me. The song is called "Lust." The lyrics say, "Hell on fire. Lust, desire. The devil wants to stick you. The devil wants to lick you. He wants your body. He wants your spirit. Naked twisting bodies, sweating. Prince of darkness. Prince of evil. Spread your legs and scream. This is no dream. Degradation. Humiliation. Thrusting, shoving. Animals humping. He is like a dog in heat. You are just another piece of meat. Craving demons fill you with pain. Now you are bloodied and stained, hurt and beaten. He will possess you. He will molest you. Sex with Satan. Sex with Satan."

While we will not consider the subject in depth at this time, it should be noted that occultic themes, primarily Satanism, is prevalent among such bands as Slayer, Venom, and Merciful Fate, one of whose albums is shown in this picture.

Let us move on to sexuality, a theme which has been part of rock music since its beginning. Today's rock artists are describing sexual activity and practice in terms more graphic than ever before. Many of you are aware of Purple Rain, the multimillion seller by Prince. Much has been said about the song "Darling Nikki" from the album. "I met a girl named Nikki. I guess you could say she was a sex fiend. I met her in a hotel lobby masturbating with magazines." Another album by Prince called "Dirty Mind" presents a positive attitude toward the subject of incest.

These lyrics are from the song called "Sister." "I was only 16, but I guess that is no excuse.

My sister was 32, and kind of alone. My sister never made love to anyone but me. Incest is everything it's said to be."

This is the cover of the album "Stakk Attakk" by the band Wrath Child. The back cover of this album, which is available to young children in record stores, included this photo of a nude woman on the back of the album. Songs include "Sweet Surrender." "I lick my lips and make advances. You lay on down and let me in. But you can't fight. You've got no choice. I will take you down and rub my cream in."

Another song on an earlier album called "Cock Rock Shock" said the words "We are going to fuck you" and "Oh, you fucking little bitch."

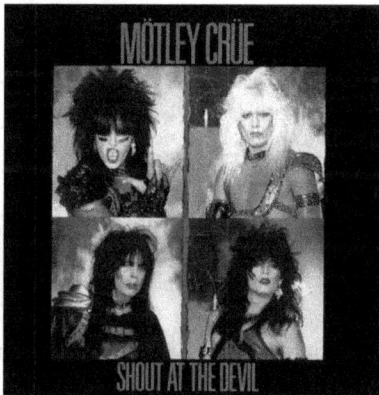

This is Motley Crue's album, "Shout at the Devil," double platinum. The song on the album we are concerned with here is "Ten Seconds to Love." "Touch my gun, but don't pull my trigger. Shine my pistol some more. Here I come. Reach down real low. Slide it in real slow. You feel so good. Do you want some more? I have got one more shot. My gun is still warm."

The band *KISS*, popular with young people, "At All Times," their brand new album, was released just yesterday, includes songs such as "Fits Like a Glove." "Ain't a cardinal sin, baby. Let me in. Girl, I am going to treat you right. Well, goodness sakes, my snake's alive, and it is ready to bite. Baby, let me in. It fits like a glove. I think I am going to burst. When I go through her it is like a hot knife through butter."

And the song, "Give Me More." "Hot blood, need your love. Hard as rock, can't get enough. Want to feel you deep inside, pumping through my veins. Fill you to the core, like a dog to the bone. Make you sweat, make you moan. Come on, lick my candy cane."

This is Betsy. She is the lead singer of a band called *Bitch*. The album is called "Be My Slave." It is available in record stores.

One of the songs is called "Give Me a Kiss." "The way you grab me makes my knees shake. The way you pull my arms makes my body quake. The way you yank my hair, it just makes me want to kill you. I will take off my clothes. Kick me in the shins. Come on and slap me in the face, and I will get down on my knees and move you like this."

And the song "Leatherbound." "The whip is my toy. Handcuffs are your joy. You hold me down, and I am screaming for more. When you tie me up and gag me, the way you give me pain, come on, give me lashes."

The Rolling Stones on their album "Under Cover" also sang of sadomasochistic activities in the song "Tie You Up." "The pain of love, you dream of it, passion it. You even get a rise from it. Feel the hot come dripping on your thigh from it. Why so divine, the pain of love." Even the *Jacksons'* mainstream pop music today, their song, "Torture," was released as a video, and was shown on national TV. That video included pictures of women dressed in leather bondage, masks, with whips in their hands, in chains, and wrapped up in handcuffs.

Some artists take their pornograph rock to the stage. This is a picture of Wendy O'Williams in

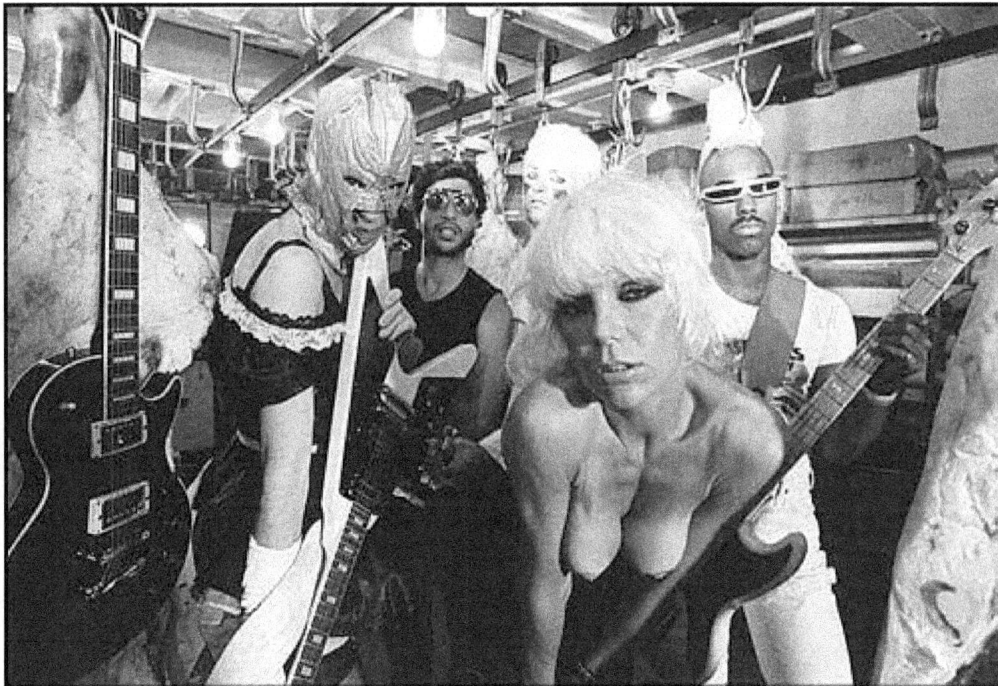

concert. Concerts that young adolescents can attend. *

[End of slide presentation.]

Mr. LING. How bad can it get? The list is endless. This album was released just recently by a band called the Mentors. It was released in an album with the label Enigma Records, which also launched *Motley Crue's* career. The album includes songs like "Four-F Club," "Find Her, Feel Her, Fuck Her, and Forget Her," "Free Fix for a Fuck," "Clap Queen," "My Erection is

* It was actually Wendy O. Williams not Wendy O'Williams. Williams first attempted suicide in 1993 by hammering a knife into her chest where it lodged in her sternum. However, she changed her mind and called Swenson to take her to the hospital. She attempted suicide again in 1997 with an overdose of ephedrine.

Williams died of self-inflicted gunshot wound on April 6, 1998, when she was 48. Rod Swenson, who had been Wendy's significant other for more than 20 years, returned to their home in a wooded area where they had lived since moving to Connecticut from New York. He found a package that Wendy left him with some special noodles he liked, a packet of seeds for growing garden greens, some oriental massage balm and sealed letters from Wendy. The suicide letters which included a "living will" denying life support, a love letter to Swenson and various lists of things to do which caused Swenson to begin searching the woods for her. After about an hour, when it was almost dark, he found her body in a woody area where she loved to feed the wildlife. Several nut shells were on a nearby rock where she had apparently been feeding some of the squirrels before she died. Swenson checked the body for a pulse, and there was none. A pistol lay on the ground nearby, and he returned to the house to call the local authorities. "Wendy's act was not an irrational in-the-moment act," he said, she had been talking about taking her own life for almost four years.

Over," and the song "Golden Showers," which says these words, "Listen, you little slut, do as you are told, come with daddy for me to pour the gold. Golden showers. All through my excrement you shall roam. Bend up and smell my anal vapor . Your face is my toilet paper. On your face I leave a shit tower. Golden showers."

Mr. Chairman, that concludes my remarks. I thank you.

[The materials referred to follow:]

[From the *Los Angeles Times*, Aug. 25, 1985]
PARENTS WARN: TAKE THE SEX AND SHOCK OUT OF ROCK
(By Patrick Goldstein)

When Susan Baker was in high school, she used to go out dancing on the weekends at a club called the *Teenage Retreat*. "It was a neat place," she said. "They played all sorts of great rock 'n' roll - Chuck Berry, Elvis, Buddy Holly and Fats Domino. We always had a good time."

Today, rock has changed and so has Baker. She's a mother of "a big batch of kids," including a 7 year old daughter, and she's "shocked" by the transformation that rock has undergone since the days when Elvis caused an uproar by swiveling his hips on "The Ed Sullivan Show." In fact, as vice president of the Washington based Parents Music Resource Center (PMRC), she's in the forefront of the fight to clean up rock, a battle that has seen PMRC leaders denounce such popular performers as Prince, Sheena Easton Madonna, *Judas Priest* and *Twisted Sister*.

"We're telling parents that they've got to wake up and see what's going on," said Baker in a phone interview. "Rock is much more sexually explicit than it was even 10 years ago. The fringe has become the mainstream. Bands like *Motley Crue, Twisted Sister* and *W.A.S.P.* are on the cover of *Hit Parader* teen magazine these days. "Have you heard the lyrics to 'Sugar Walls' (a million selling hit single written by Prince and recorded by Sheena Easton earlier this year)? They go: "The blood races to your private spots, lets me know there's a fire, can't fight passion when passion is hot, temperatures rise inside my sugar walls."

"And you should hear the way she sings those lyrics, using this very sexy, erotic voice," Baker said, putting extra emphasis on the word erotic. "Well, you don't have to be much older than 10 to know what she means."

To attract the record industry's attention, the center has waged a high profile media campaign, which has seen its members widely quoted in the national press as well as making appearances on such influential programs as "Today" and "Donahue."

The center has another important weapon at its disposal. The group, widely known in the press as the "Washington wives," is headed by the spouses of several prominent senators and Reagan Administration officials. Baker, for example, is married to Treasury Secretary James Baker. The group's other vice president is Tipper Gore, wife of Sen. Albert Gore Jr. (D Tenn.). Led by President Pam Howar (wife of a Washington construction firm executive), the centre's membership also includes Nancy Thurmond, the wife of Sen. Strom Thurmond (R S.C.), as well as the spouses of several other congressional leaders.

The center wields considerable political clout. Last year, the PTA's national leadership requested that the music industry label records for profanity or sexual content, a plea that was widely ignored. But barely four months after the center was formed, it has won significant concessions from Stan Gortikov, president of the Recording Industry Assn. of America (RIAA), who pledged that record companies will put labels on albums to warn parents and children about potentially offensive and sexually explicit lyrics.

A key question, which most record industry leaders refuse to discuss – at least on the record – is whether the record association's swift acquiescence was prompted, in part, by the industry's fear that a nationwide debate over bawdy rock lyrics could affect the industry's campaign for government legislation protecting it against record piracy, copyright violations and granting record companies royalties from the sale of blank tapes.

The proposed legislation could eventually come to a vote before the Senate Judiciary Committee, now chaired by Sen. Thurmond. The nine member Senate Communications Subcommittee, of which Sen. Gore is a member, has already announced that it will hold a hearing on the controversy over rock lyrics next month.

RIAA officials stopped short of accusing the PMRC of throwing around its collective political weight. "They haven't made any direct threats, at least to my knowledge," said RIAA spokeswoman Patricia Heimers. However, she quickly added, "Let's put it this way – the PMRC leaders haven't been at all reluctant to make known their political connections."
"You bet it's helped," Baker said. "There's no doubt that it's played

a part in helping us get some attention. However, there's no quid pro quo here. But let me tell you this - there are an awful lot of parents in Washington, D.C., in politics and other areas, that are very upset by the blatant sexuality and raunchy, explicit language in rock today."

The few record executives willing to discuss this political connection tried to downplay its significance. "I don't see this affecting any of our legislative efforts," said MCA Records President Irving Azoff. "I can't imagine any linkage - separate issues are separate issues."

However, outspoken pop star Frank Zappa isn't so sure.

"The RIAA didn't agree to this stickering of albums on moral grounds, but business ones," he said. "The industry has a huge financial interest in anti home taping and piracy legislation. And guess who runs the committee that oversees this legislation? Sen. Strom Thurmond, whose wife is a member of the PMRC. I think the connection's pretty clear. The record companies are willing to chop up artists' civil rights so that they won't have to lose any potential profits from their anti home taping and piracy campaign."

Pop lyrics have always been subject to censorship, for real - or imagined - sexual content. A recently published list of songs that had been banned at one time or another include such now established standards as Rodgers and Hart's "Bewitched," Cole Porter's "Love for Sale," Irving Berlin's "Heat Wave" and Cahn and De Paul's "Teach Me Tonight."

But today's songs are clearly more explicit, some too explicit to be printed in a family newspaper. Berlin lead singer Terri Nunn has sung, "You can buy me a daiquiri, you can take me home and tear my clothes off." Heavy metal veterans *Kiss* bellow, "Burn bitch, burn." Even Marvin Gaye, who once sang mellow ballads like "Your Precious Love," made a posthumous appearance on the charts this year with a song called "Sanctified Lady," which referred to women as "nasty little slaves" and contained graphic sexual images.

The biggest offender, according to PMRC leaders, is Prince, who has penned lyrics about such raunchy topics as oral sex, masturbation and incest. The song that angry parents mention the most - "Darling Nikki," from Prince's Granny and Oscar winning album, "Purple Rain" - describes "Nikki" as a "sex fiend" who arouses herself by reading sex magazines.

Even Bruce Springsteen, the '80s All American boy who has been embraced by such political heavyweights as President Reagan and Sen. Bill Bradley (D N.J.), has been criticized by the PMRC for promoting loose sex. As Howar told one interviewer - referring to Springsteen's recent hit, "I'm On Fire" - "Even Bruce isn't clean."

According to Baker, her involvement with PMRC began when she hear her 7 year old daughter singing along to hit songs by Madonna that she had heard on her clock radio. "While those songs are basically more suggestive than explicit, it awakened me to what's going on in pop music today," said Baker, who said her other children are either grown or off at college. "I think parents have a responsibility, instead of telling kids to turn down the music, to listen to what the music is saying.

"Cole Porter used suggestive music, sure. But those were double entendres aimed at a mature audience. Now we're hearing songs about pure sex and even forced rape that are geared toward kids. I've walked into a record store and seen an album cover with a naked girl whose body has been painted blue, with her genital area covered with a chain and a lock. Now I don't think my 7 year old should see that flipping through records in a store."

With that in mind, the PMRC has launched a campaign to clean up the record business. Its stated goals include: album jacket warning stickers, inclusion of lyrics on all album jackets and a move to put albums with explicit album covers under the counters at record stores. The group has also asked that record companies exert pressure on broadcasters not to air explicit records and music videos as well as reassess the contracts of pop stars who display violence or sexual behavior in concert.

After several meetings in recent months with industry leaders, the RIAA announced recently that it will have record companies put labels on albums to warn parents and children about potentially offensive and sexually explicit lyrics. However, the PMRC is still not satisfied. "We were pleased to see the record association agree to a generic warning," Baker said. "But we'd like an official panel, consisting of industry executives and community officials, who would set up general guidelines for industry standards."

RIAA chief Gortikov refused to comment on the continuing negotiations. However, RIAA spokeswoman Heimers, who criticized the center's "strident press campaign," said that the association has "rejected" the idea of an advisory panel.

Many record company chieftains, including Warner Bros. President Lenny Waroner, CBS Records Chairman Walter Yetnikoff, EMI President Jim Mazza and Elektra President Bob Krasnow, as well as top executives at PolyGram and Atlantic Records, refused to comment on the issue, preferring to let the record association speak for them.

However, the uproar has prompted many industry leaders to lambast the center for applying rigid standards to song lyrics that are so ambiguous that they can be interpreted in many ways.
"I can't believe they're serious - I think this whole thing is ridiculous," said Jay Boberg, 27 year old president of I.R.S. Records. "I would fight to the death any review board that would rate our records. It's a complete intrusion of artistic expression and constitutional freedom of speech. It would be a very dark day if we were ever forced to go along with anything like that."

Boberg insisted that any ratings system would merely encourage kids to seek out albums that carried a warning tag. "When you put ratings on things, it just arouses kids' curiosity and makes them want to hear them all the more. That's what happened with the movie ratings. I know that when I was 16, which wasn't so long ago, if a movie was rated R, that just whetted my appetite to see what I was missing."

"The whole nature of rock has always been the double entendre - that's what has made it so alluring and intriguing," said A&M President Gil Friesen. "What it comes down to is that we're a democratic society and the freedom of options that comes with that is not something to be taken lightly."

Other execs feel the PMRC move would set a dangerous precedent. "There is too much glamorization of drug use and sexual license," said Geffen Records President Eddie Rosenblatt. "But what's the next step — are you going to regulate controversial political ideas or philosophical ones?

Rock music doesn't make these things happen, it mirrors what you see in society. A rock song never made any kid want to go out and get laid."

Frank Zappa was also critical of the whole record rating campaign. "The whole thing is preposterous — it seems like the kind of campaign a bored Washington housewife would dream up when she's at a summer barbecue," he said. "The record industry is acting like of bunch of cowards. They're scared to death of the fundamentalist right and want to throw them a bone in hopes that they'll go away.

But this stickering program   will just start a precedent—
they'll always want more."

Other record execs seem to view the center   as Keystone Kops style
adversaries. "I just wish that Prince was on my label so I could
have all these problems," quipped MCA Records President Azoff.

Speaking more seriously, Azoff added, "I think it's really
unfortunate that at a time when pop figures have been in the
forefront of so many important causes, like Live Aid and USA for
Africa, that this kind of issue is getting so much media attention."

Many industry leaders have complained that rock n' roll is being
singled out for attack when sex is used to sell everthing   in
America from cars and jeans to cosmetics and after shave. Is Prince
or Madonna any more suggestive than "Miami Vice" or "Dynasty"?

"We're not picking on the music industry," Baker said. "I've written
Calvin Klein to complain about his ads, which are a debauchery. I
just flipped on the TV a few minutes ago and turned the channel to
an R rated movie with a love scene, right on daytime TV. I just
couldn't believe it.

"But we think that parents have to make their thoughts known. Did
you know that in the most recent FBI statistics, that crime in
general was down 2%, but rape was up 7%? Now, we're not blaming
that all on rock music, but it's an indication of how things are
going.

"Listen, all four of us (PMRC executives) are mothers with young
children. We're not blind - most parents today have danced to rock
n' roll and loved it. But the blatant and explicit sexuality you
hear in rock today is targeted at our children and we feel as if
it's our right to protect them."

[From the *Washington Post,* Sept. 15, 1985]
NO ONE BLUSHES ANYMORE
(By George F. Will)

Here is a question that might cause you to blush: What causes you
to blush?

When considering the campaign against "porn rock" - vulgar and
obscene lyrics in rock music - consider that question, and this one:
Would you want to live in a world in which no one, not even the

young, blushed?

Various parents' groups are putting wholesome pressure on recording companies, radio stations and the makers of rock videos to exercise discretion and self restraint. Approximately one third of the nation's radio stations have rock formats, and many are behaving responsibly.

But the sort of people who profit from aggressively marketing porn rock have the morals of the marketplace, and the marketplace is the place to get their attention. In addition, putting labels on records with vulgar lyrics is going to help parents exercise supervision.

Rock music has become a plague of messages about sexual promiscuity, bisexuality, incest, sado masochism, satanism, drug use, alcohol abuse and constantly, misogyny. The lyrics regarding these things are celebratory, encouraging or at least desensitizing. By making these subjects the common currency of popular entertainment, the lyrics drain the subjects of their power to shock - their power to make people blush. The concern is less that children will emulate the frenzied behavior described in porn rock that they they will succumb to the lassitude of the deomoralized - literally, the demoralized.

As people become older they become less given to blushing. This is, in part, because they lose that sweet softness of youthful character that is called innocence and makes one's sensibilities subject to shock. People blush for various reasons. Sometimes it is because we suddenly have embarrassing attention called to ourselves. Sometimes we blush when utterly alone, when we think of something about ourselves that is shaming - such as the fact that almost nothing causes us to blush.

Often people blush because they are exposed to something that should be private or is shameful. This may be an endangered species of blushing, thanks to omnipresent vulgarities like porn rock making even the vilest things somehow banal.

Walter Berns, the political philosopher, asks: What if, contrary to Freud and much conventional wisdom, shame is natural to man and shamelessness is acquired? If so, the acquisition of shamelessness through the shedding of "hangups" is an important political event. There is a connection between self restraint and shame. An individual incapable of shame and embarrassment is probably incapable of the governance of the self. A public incapable of shame and embarrassment about public vulgarity is unsuited to self government.

There is an upward ratchet effect in the coarsening of populations. Today's 12 year olds cannot enjoy - can hardly sit still for - the kind of 1950s Westerns that enthralled their fathers. Today's 12 year olds are so addicted (that is not too strong a word) to the slam bang nonstop roar of Steven Spielberg movies that their attention is not held by, say, John Wayne in "She Wore a Yellow Ribbon."

The social atmosphere is heavily dosed with sexuality, from the selling of blue jeans to the entertaining of prime time television audiences. Thus it is perhaps reasonable to have feelings of fatalism. Perhaps societies, like rivers, run naturally downhill. Perhaps the coarsening of a public is irreversible, especially when the coarsening concerns a powerful and pleasurable appetite such as sex. But it is demonstrably not true that societies cannot move away from coarseness toward delicacy of feeling.

In the first half of the 18th century, the dawn of the Age of Reason, a form of English merriment on Guy Fawkes nights was to burn an effigy of the Pope. The belly of the effigy was filled with cats whose howls of agony in the flames were supposed to represent the voice of the devil emanating from the Catholic Church. That kind of cruelty to animals is, by today's standards, obscene. Sensibilities can change for the better. So fatalism is wrong and the porn rock fight is worth fighting.

Mass culture, and especially music, matters. Nothing is more striking to a young parent than the pull of popular culture on even 8 and 4 year olds. And perhaps good music can make good values more adhesive to children.

People can reasonably argue about what is the second finest work of music - a Mozart concerto, a Beethoven symphony, this or that Bach tune. But everyone knows that the acme of the art of music is the currently popular song that says, "Put me in coach, I'm ready to play... Look at me, I can be center field." The republic has a fighting chance as long as the popularity of porn rock can be rivaled by the popularity of its moral opposite, baseball rock.

[From the *Christian Science Monitor*, Aug. 23, 1985]
WASHINGTON WIVES USE INFLUENCE TO TARGET SEX, DRUGS IN ROCK MUSIC
(By Julia Malone)

For years, parents have routinely shouted "Turn the music down!" over the blast of teen agers' records.

Recently a group of parents, many of whom grew up to the rock beat themselves, decided to turn the music up and listen carefully.

What they heard in the lyrics, saw on album covers, and watched on rock videos alarmed them. They joined forces and in only a few months have managed to shake, rattle, and roll the rock music industry. Their goal is a rating system for records and videos similar to the G, PG, R, or X now applied to movies.

This group, which includes wives of some of the most powerful men in Washington, is getting action. They charge some popular songs, which endorse violence, bestiality, and even incest, are blatant pornography.

"A line of decency has been crossed," says Susan Baker, wife of Treasury Secretary James A. Baker III, and a co founder last May of the Parents' Music Resource Center   (PMRC).
Critics concede that lyrics about sex and drugs are not new; such themes were found in the songs of Cole Porter, Billie Holiday, and the *Beatles.*

The difference today, say PMRC members, is in degree and in the target audience. Madonna who is seductively posed on the cover of her album "Like a Virgin," wearing a belt buckle carrying the words "Boy Toy," attracts mostly preteen fans.

The double entendres of the 1960s and '70s have given way to graphic descriptions of sex and violence. Brutality to women and satanic worship are common themes.

PMRC members concede that such music is only a small part of the rock scene. Mary Elizabeth (Tipper) Gore, wife of Sen. Albert Gore Jr. (D) of Tennessee and a founder of PMRC, observes, "I love rock music; I still am a consumer of it." But she says that some current rock depicts "sadomasochism, killing, raping, as an apparently normal way to relate to women."

PMRC is taking its message to the public. Members are appearing on television talk shows and presenting copies of explicit lyrics to top music executives.

"The fact that we are in Washington and are married to important men has certainly helped our cause," says Mrs. Baker. But the founders did not expect the tidal wave of public interest, including more than 10,000 letters from parents and teenagers and nonstop phone calls.

"I absolutely had no idea this was an issue waiting to be born," says Pam Howar, the group's president and wife of a top Washington real estate developer.

The music industry is responding with alacrity and some grumbling.

So far 19 recording companies have agreed to put the warning "parental guidance: explicit lyrics" on selected records. Buyers will see them in stores "in a couple of months," says a spokesman for the Recording Industry Association of America.

The National Association of Broadcasters has alerted its member rock stations. By some accounts, program managers are beginning to screen music more carefully. PMRC has been invited to present its case at the NAB convention in Dallas Sept. 12.

PMRC has also sparked a congressional hearing for Sept. 18 before a Senate Commerce subcommittee. Although the subcommittee says the hearing is for "information only," music industry spokesmen note that husbands of PMRC members are members of the panel. Gary Stevens, president of Doubleday Broadcasting and overseer of rock stations in six cities, has become one of the few outspoken critics of PMRC. He opposes its campaign as a first step toward censorship, which could prevent some records and videos from being broadcast. "Who knows where it stops?" he says. "Once the labels are on, they're going to be all over us."

Mrs. Howar, of the Parents Music Resource Workshop, confirms those fears. "I think they're going to find they have to respond to community pressure," she says. While PMRC has stirred activity, its founders are far from satisfied. The "parental guidance" label falls short of their goal of formation of a panel, composed of music industry and community members, to set uniform criteria for warning labels. PMRC also wants the label to read "R," for restricted.

"It's a truth in packaging type issue," says Mrs. Gore. If each record company sets different standards for labels, it will "confuse the consumer," she says.

Gore discovered the need for warnings when her 12 year old daughter asked to buy "Purple Rain," a hit album by superstar Prince. "All I knew was that Prince was a new figure on the scene," she says, adding that she had liked one of his songs on the radio.

Once her daughter brought "Purple Rain" home, Gore heard a song that began, "I knew [a girl named Nikki/I guess you could say she was a sex fiend," followed by a graphic sexual description. The album was immediately remanded to an upper shelf.

PMRC makes no apologies for shocking other parents, public officials, and music executives who seldom listen to rock music. On its list of unacceptable lyrics are words from the group *Motley Crue's* top selling "Shout at the Devil' album: "...now I'm killing you...Watch your face turning blue."

They also point to a Prince album entitled "Dirty Mind" that praises incest as "everything it's said to be."

The trickle of explicit language in rock has become a river, says the Rev. Jeff Ling, a minister, rock music expert, and consultant to PMRC.

"Kids have a very difficult problem with self image as it is," he says, adding that problems increase when they see "mankind at its most base."

"All of society is saturated" with such messages, he concedes. But like his fellow activists, he says that "you can only tackle one issue at a time." He says they are choosing rock music because it is aimed at preteens and teens.

The group calculated that the average teen ager listens to such music five hours a day, or 10,000 hours during Grades 7 through 12.

Bill Steding, general manager of Central Broadcasting in Dallas, says he's expecting a "lot more receptivity" from radio programmers at the broadcasters' convention next month. He says he has noticed stations already becoming more "conservative."

"Even radio stations didn't listen very well to the lyrics" in the past, he says. "Now they've started to pay attention."

His rock station, KAFM in Dallas, has long had strict rules about sex, violence, and drugs in music. "We edit or do not play certain songs," Mr. Steding says. At the same time, the station is one of the top five in the city.

"We just took a position...that we wanted to have a positive impact on teens," he says.

He adds that a recent survey found that policy helped the station's popularity. The survey indicated that listeners who most objected to explicit or violent music were 15 to 18 year olds.

[From *Billboard*, June 29, 1985]
A CALL FOR SELF-RESTRAINT -- PORN ROCK: A SCRIPT FOR CENSORSHIP
(By George David Weiss)

Censorship, a hydra headed insatiable beast, is crouching in the shadows ready to pounce upon and consume our music industry. The cause? Violent and sexually explicit rock lyrics permeating our airwaves and invading our videos.

Some signposts:

The national office of the Parent Teachers Assn. has requested record companies to rate their product, as is done by the movie industry.

The National Assn. of Broadcasters has asked record companies to include lyric sheets with records sent to stations. It has also written to more than 800 radio and television group station owners asking each licensee to decide the manner in which is should carry out its "programming responsibilities" under the Communications Act.

The Parents Music Resource Center, co chaired by Susan Baker and Tipper Gore, the respective spouses of Treasury Secretary Jim Baker, and Sen. Albert Gore of Tennessee, is asking the music industry to establish a rating system to both inform and warn consumers of the content in the product they purchase. This is particularly for the benefit of parents who are concerned about the lyrics their kids listen to.

The Rev. Jesse Jackson has gone to the extreme of suggesting that record companies accept at least some responsibility for the high rate of black teenage pregnancy.

We shouldn't adopt a head in the sand attitude about these developments. They are danger signals that a storm is brewing. Before the deluge we should seed these ominous clouds with common sense, perhaps thereby rendering them harmless.

Now—not later— is the time to open a dialog with each other in the hope that responsible leaders can help avoid the disaster to which inaction must inevitably lead.

Throughout the ages it has been acknowledged that music has the power to do more than entertain. It can ennoble and inspire; it can form character. It saddens one to see it so often appeal to the basest in use , rather than the best. I refer here specifically to the phenomenon that is rising so rapidly: porn rock.

Where lyrics once used innuendo, they are now overt.

Where lyrics once were artfully suggestive, they are now blatantly explicit.

Where lyrics once extolled tenderness and love relationships, they now glorify violence and loveless sex.

"What's the big deal?" ask some. "There are porno theatres all over the country, aren't there?"

That's true, of course. And even a growing percentage of "legitimate" movies provide a steady stream of four letter words and gratuitous sex scenes.

The difference, though is that no one is breaking your arm to buy a ticket to the movies. It's your choice. But the airwaves? That's a horse of a distinctly different color.

The public has no control over what is beamed into its homes. Preteeners are being exposed to a rising tide of openly libidinous suggestions they are yet ill equipped to deal with. And adults (even if they could decipher the lyrics) can hardly be expected to sit by day and night monitoring what comes through speaker and tube.

Have we forgotten that the airwaves belong to the people? The right to use these airwaves is merely on loan, so to speak, to licensees.

Certainly, the majority of parents, if asked, would vote overwhelmingly against their kids hearing or viewing songs that recommend masturbation, oral sex, intercourse in elevators, violence, Satanism, sado masochism and other such pastimes.

The trick, of course, is never to reach the point where parents are asked to vote, or where government decides to intervene.

I submit that the only sensible course of action is industrywide self restraint. Songwriters, using their conscience as their guide, should tone down on explicitness. Publishers should edit lyrics more carefully. Producers and record companies should exercise more responsibility over what is or isn't recorded. Singers should use better judgment in choosing their material. And finally, broadcasters should become more aware of what they are transmitting.

I suspect there are many who disagree with some or much of the above. That's all the more reason for a reasonable debate to take place - but quickly, while it still remains reasonable.

A powerful array of artists raised many millions of dollars with their recording of "We Are The World." They did this out of concern and anguish over the physical health (indeed, the lives) of children in Africa.

But what about the moral health of children in America, or elsewhere in the world? Aren't their emotional health and developing values also worth our attention?

If those same artists who have so dramatically shown what a dedicated joint effort can accomplish were now to focus on this burgeoning problem, their influence could go a long way toward shutting off the spigot of tasteless, blatantly sexual lyrics, and the shockingly graphic videos saturating the TV channels. There is surely enough violence in our society without glorifying it in the music aimed at our youngsters.

This would be a far more palatable method of restoring sanity and subtlety to songs than the dangerous alternative—censorship.

[From the *Washington Post*, June 19, 1985]
FILTH ON THE AIR
(By William Raspberry)

A group of Washington women, including the wives of some of the city's most powerful men, may be about to do for our children what we couldn't – or wouldn't – do for them ourselves. They're about to clean up their air.

The polluters these women have in mind are not the smokestack industry but the record industry. Like us, they are sick of the filth that passes for lyrics on some of the most popular records, tapes and videos. Unlike us, they are prepared to move—have moved, in fact.

Mrs. Albert Gore, Jr. (he's the Tennessee senator) and Mrs. James A. Baker III (he's the Treasury secretary) are no blue nose record smashers. They are mothers who are distressed that their children are being exposed to a filth, violence, sadomasochism and explicit sex whenever they switch on their favorite radio station or watch televised videos. They aren't demanding censorship; they want a choice.

As a very minimum, they want the record industry to label their products after the style of the movie industry, so that at least they and their children know what they are buying. As it is now, you can't always tell.

Tipper Gore, mother of four, found out the hard way, when her 11 year old daughter came home with Prince's "Purple Rain." "She bought it because she liked 'Let's Go Crazy,' but then I heard the words to 'Darling Nikki,' with its lyrics about a girl masturbating with a magazine, and I started paying attention.

"Then I happened to talk with Susan Baker, whom I had met through an international club we both belong to, and I found out she was going through the same thing with her children. We got together with Pam Howar [whose husband is a construction executive [, Sally Nevius [her husband, Jack, is a former chairman of the D.C. City Council and Ethelann Stuckey [wife of the former Florida congressman and decided to try to do something about it.

They formed the Parents Music Resource Center and managed to swing enough clout to get Stan Gortikov, president of the Recording Industry Association of America, to come down from New York to meet with them. They also persuaded Edward Fritts, president of the National Association of Broadcasters, to ask 45 recording companies to supply written lyrics for their albums so that broadcasters can know what they are playing.

That may help, though surely the deejays must be aware that "Bitch, Be My Slave" is not exactly what parents want their pre teens to listen to.

"The children really don't have a choice," Tipper Gore says. "They flip through the record bin and they see a cover with a nude woman gagged and chained to a motorcycle, or another one simulating maturbation with a light bulb. There's one record—platinum, yet—with a song called 'Eat Me Alive' that is about oral sex at gunpoint. Some of it I can't bring myself to talk about. It's simply gone too far, and it has to be stopped; at least we have a right to know what's on an album so we can exercise some control."

Much of the filth and depravity is, if the youngsters are to be believed, purely gratuitous. They say it is the melody and the beat that are the principal attractions, and that they would still choose many of the same records if the lyrics were far milder.

As things stand, the children have no realistic choice. It's impossible to listen to most of the rock stations, or watch the televised videos, without being exposed to kinky sex, torture and even killing.

Some of it, no doubt, is calculated to shock. But because we adults, in our pseudosophistication, refuse to acknowledge shock, the effect is to legitimize and popularize things that ought to have us screaming bloody murder.

Now, thanks to a handful of Washington women, maybe we'll take our heads out of the sand and start screaming.

[From the *Washington Post*, Sept. 14, 1985]
ROCK RATINGS
(By Ellen Goodman)

BOSTON.—There is something familiar about the scene. A public
conflict between concerned mothers in silk and outrageous rock
stars in skin. A People magazine cover with a shopworn
headline: "Has Rock Gone too Far?" A meeting with broadcasters
this week, a congressional hearing next week, furrowed brows, lips
that roll the words "Sex, Violence, Rock 'n' Roll" into one.

Haven't we been here before? How many times before? Which side
were we on before? Surely the Golden Oldies among us titter over
memories of the Movement to Restore Decency, the midnight record
burners, the prudes who televised Elvis only from the waist up.
"They" as Elvis said, "are just frustrated old types anyway." And
we were inclined to agree.

Rock was born and bred to be anti establishment and despite the
news that Ringo Starr has become a grandfather, yesterday's
rocker to loathe become today's establishment. But even the most
terminally tolerant of rock fans knows that something has
happened since the days of the old hound dog.

The outrageous edge of rock and roll has shifted its focus from
Elvis' pelvis to the saw protruding from Blackie Lawless'
codpiece on a *W.A.S.P.* album. Rock lyrics have turned from "I can't
get no satisfaction" to "I'm going to force you at gunpoint to
eat me alive."
The veritable Prince of rock is now writing ballads to
his sister—"Incest is everything they said it would be" — and
Motley Crue has become the bard of rape—"I'll either break her
face or take down her legs." You do not have to be a "frustrated
old type" to hope that your children don't go around the house
singing the words to "Nightstalker."

It's this heavy metal message that is forcing an older generation
of fans to become critics. One of them, Tipper Gore, 36, wife of
Sen. Al Gore (D Tenn.), mother of four and Phil Collins fan, is one
of those who said "enough." She and Susan Baker, wife of Treasury
Secretary Jim Baker, with two others formed something called the
Parents Music Resource Center . They have had as much publicity
lately as Madonna.

The women of the PMRC have been attacked with such lethal

epithets as "Washington wives," "ladies" and, gasp, "housewives," as if they were swinging pocketbooks at the heads of rock stars. Indeed some in the industry portray the "wives" and their allies in the PTA as right wing censors out to limit the free speech of the whole motley crew.

Frankly, I think it would be lovely if all the broadcasters, producers and musicians had the restraint to limit the amount of mayhem that went out over the airwaves. You cannot direct "adult" songs specifically into 15 and over eardrums. The lyrics drift, like cigarette smoke, polluting everyone within range, doing the worst to the youngest.

But the goal of this group is really quite modest. They are not trying to censor the *W.A.S.P.*, ban the Twisted Sister, or inflict pain and suffering on the Torture Rock crowd. Their primary aim is to get a label on the rock music records, to win a consumer victory for parents. They would also like to brown bag the worst of the porn covers and to get the raunchiest lyrics out front so the buyer could beware.

PMRC has not been without effect. This summer, the record industry agreed to a mild PG rating, providing that each company rate its own artists. But PG sounds a bit too much like "okay." The PMRC would like a single industry wide standard and an R. The PTA, for its part, would like more specific ratings.

I have reservations about ratings, though not the same ones the record companies have. The movie experience is mixed at best. Under the cover of an R, the amount of violence has actually increased. The ratings are often arbitrary (four letter words are more of a no no than chain saw murders), and there is nothing like a dirty rumor to boost sales. But ratings are a better guide than what parents had before: nothing.

Ratings are nothing more or less than a modest way of reintroducing something called standards. It is a way the collective community of adults can say, "We disapprove." We disapprove of violence, we disapprove of sexual exploitation. We do not want our pre teens to watch the *W.A.S.P.* smashing the head of a woman in chains.

Does that make us the establishment? Does that mean our kids will rebel? Frankly, it doesn't really matter. What does matter is that we let our children know what we think.

[From the *Esquire*, May 1984]
AMERICAN -- WORDS OF LOVE -- FROM TODAY'S TEENAGERS, A DIFFERENT KIND OF FAN MAIL
(By Bob Greene)

Traveling   through Texas, I listened to local radio stations. In San Antonio I found myself listening to KISS FM, a rock 'n' roll outlet.

On the air, one of the station's disc jockeys mentioned a promotion. "What would you do to meet the *Crüe?* he said. He explained that a heavy metal rock band called *Mötley Crüe* was coming to San Antonio. Listeners were invited to mail entries to the station. The winners would get free tickets to the concert; some would get to go backstage and meet the band.
I called the station. I said I would be interested in seeing the entries. I asked if there were any ground rules. I was told that the only rule was that listeners had to answer the one basic question: "What would you do to meet the *Crüe?* ["

A week later, I read the entries.

We seem to have come quite a distance from *Herman's Hermits* fan clubs and "I Want to Hold Your Hand."

From a sixteen year old girl:

"What I Would Do To See *Mötley Crüe.*

"First, I would tie you up, spread eagle and naked, with leather straps. Then I'd shave all the hair off of your chest, and if I should nick you I'll suck up all the blood as it slowly trickles over your body. Next I'll cover your body with motion lotion to get things really heated up. When it gets too hot, I'll cover your body in crushed ice and lay on top of you to melt it down and cool you off.

"Then I'll do things to your body with my tongue that you never thought humanly possible. Then when you are screaming for mercy and begging for more, telling me how you want it all, I'll slam the spiked heel of my right leather boot into your navel, call you a very naughty boy, and laugh as I slowly walk away, telling you I'm just not that kind of girl."

From a fifteen year old girl:

"I want to see *Mötley Crüe* so bad I'd wear black nail polish and body glitter. . . . When I see them I'd get on may hands & knees & give them my body & even tear my clothes off if I had to. If that didn't work I'd do like Ozzy did and bite a dove's head off & say, 'Okay, let's talk business.' "

From a thirteen year old girl:

"I'd do it with the *Crüe* till black and blue is all you can see."

From a fifteen year old girl:

"I'm really a big fan *of Mötley Crüe's* and I would do anything to meet them. Vince Neil and Nikki Sixx are so fine! I love 'em all. I would even get fucked by the ugliest, fattest, most disgusting guy in the world to meet them...

"My boyfriend gets mad at me because I like them so much, and listen to the radio all the time for their songs to come on! I had to beg him to let me write this letter to you. Hopefully, I will win, because I went through a lot of trouble begging my boyfriend to let me do this.

"That would be just terrific if I won. I would have a chance of meeting Vince Neil! God. [, he's so fucking fine! If it would mean losing my boyfriend. I would fuck his best friend to meet these gorgeous guys. It wouldn't matter, as long as I got to meet Vince Neil and see his fine ass and fine body! God, I can just see it now. Fucking him would be my biggest fantasy in the world! Well, I hope I win! Thank you!"

From a thirteen year old girl:

"I'd leave my tits to *Mötley Crüe.*"

From a seventeen year old girl:

"To get backstage to *Mötley Crüe* I think I'd give them every piece of action they wanted. I'd give them my body, money, or whatever they wanted."

From a nineteen year old girl:

"I would go down to the local hardware store and buy some chains, leather straps, and nails. I would then put together the most outlandish outfit made of nothing but the leather straps, chains and nails. I would go to the concert in this Kiss Ass outfit, because I would do anything to get close to 'Marvelous' Mick Mars, 'Luscious' Tommy Lee, Nikki 'Sixx,' and Vince 'Can't say No' Neil. P.S. I would take a hammer so the guys (the *Crüe*) can loosen the nails in my outfit."

From a thirteen year old girl:

"What's up? Well, you asked what I would do to be *a Mötley Crüe*, so here it is. First, I'd spread whipped cream all over my body. Then I'd let Vince Neil lick it all off! I sure hope you enjoyed this cause I would love for it to happen."

From a fourteen year old boy:

This is what I would do to join the *KISS Mötley Crüe*. I would give them my mother, who is very beautiful. She has red hair and brown eyes. She loves heavy metal and especially *Mötley Crüe*. My mother definitely has the looks that kill.

I spoke with the sixteen year old girl who said she would tie the band members up with leather straps and shave their chests.

"I didn't let my boyfriend read it before I sent it in," she said. "It would make him wonder what he didn't know about me."

"Why did I write those things? I don't know. I just sat down and wrote what I thought. It took me about half an hour, I don't know where the ideas came from. They just came out."
I spoke with the girl's mother.

"Yes, I read the letter," the mother said, "Actually, I took it down to the radio station for her. I guess I was shocked in a way, but I'm sure she didn't mean anything by it. She's a very Christian girl.

"Did I think about not turning it in to the radio station? Well, it really wouldn't have been fair for me not to turn it in. I promised my daughter I would do it. It wouldn't have been fair for me to put it in the garbage.'

I spoke with the fifteen year old girl who said she would get on her hands and knees for the band and give them her body.

"I was one of the winners of the contest, but I didn't get to go to the concert because I didn't have a ride," she said. "My father was supposed to take me, but he had to work late. I didn't speak to him for two days.

"I meant what I said. I'd get on my hands and knees and give them my body. I know that they're grown men and I'm fifteen, but so what? It would be worth giving them my body just to meet them. I think it would be neat.

"I heard that in ancient time women use to get on their hands and knees and not even be allowed to look at men. I think rock groups should be treated like that. They're like God, but they're even better. The reason I would take my clothes off and crawl to them is that I would hope that they like that."

I spoke with the thirteen year old girl who said she would do "it" with the band until she was black and blue.

"I just love the group," she said. "I wrote what I wrote because they look like the type who would like that. They look like women lovers."

I spoke with the fifteen year old girl who said she would go to bed with "the ugliest, fattest, most disgusting guy in the world" in order to meet the band.

"I like their hair," she said. "I just like them a lot. It's pretty boring in this town. I don't like school very much, I get Cs and Ds. I wrote those things because I thought it might help me win. I meant every word of it.

"I really like Vince Neil's body. When he's onstage he wears a bunch of spikes and leather pants. I'd do whatever I had to do to meet him. I told my mother's bodyfriend about it, and he said, 'Whatever turns you on.' "

I spoke with the thirteen year old girl who said she would "leave my tits" to the band.

"I really like the way their faces look," she said. "It makes me excited to see them onstage.

"I wrote what I did because I thought they might like it, and then I'd get to meet them. You can tell that they're like that. All rock groups know that they can have any girls' bodies that they want. That's one of the reasons they join a band."

I spoke with the seventeen year old girl who said she would give the band "every piece of action they wanted," and give the band money.

"They seem like a wild, outgoing bunch of guys to me," she said. "They seem like they'd do just about anything and not care about it.

"I'd give them whatever they wanted. They can do whatever they want with my body. They look wild and mean and evil. What I meant about giving them money is that first I'd try to convince them in other ways to take my body. I'd follow them where they went and tell them to do with me whatever they wanted to. I think I could convince them.

"But if they wanted money for it, I'd pay them to take me. It would be worth the money to me. I have some money saved from baby sitting; plus my father is a truck driver, and I could borrow the money from him if I needed more.

"I'd do it with all four of them at once if that's what they wanted. If they said, 'Be with all four of us or get out,' I'd say, 'Okay, come on.' I'd be crazy not to if that was my only chance to be with them."

I spoke with the nineteen year old girl who said she would dress in chains, leather straps, and nails for the band.

"I think they're all gorgeous," she said.

"When I see them, I just naturally think of leather and whips and chains. I think that means that they're aggressive. I happen to love that image; its a neat image.

"I think it's that kind of aggressiveness that a women is always looking for. Why did I put that thing in about bringing a hammer with me? Just like I said—they could use it to loosen the nails on my clothes."

I spoke with the thirteen year old girl who said she would let one of the band members lick whipped cream off her body.

"They're really good looking," she said.

"Good and mean. They just look like guys who are out to party and have a good time.

"I saw the band in a magazine and I thought they were pretty neat. I like Vince Neil the best of them. He's got the blondest hair; it's kind of long. He's not fat and he's not thin; he's just right.

"I wouldn't make the same offer to my boyfriend that I made to the band. It just wouldn't be the same with him. With the band, you think more of being wild and having a good time. My boyfriend is fifteen. We don't car date yet; our mothers mostly drop us off at the movies and pick us up afterward."

I spoke with the fourteen year old boy who said he would give his mother to the band.

"I wrote that letter because I really wanted to get to go backstage and meet *Mötley Crüe*," he said. "My mom likes the band, too, and I thought if I offered her to them, I might have a good chance of winning.

"If the band told me that they really wanted my mother? I'd say, 'Take her.' I'd say, 'Here.' I really love my mom; I know she'd go with them."

I spoke with the boy's mother, who is thirty four.

"Yes, I am a fan of the band," she said. "I sure am. I approved of his letter.

"We keep listening to the radio to hear their music. They're kind of wild; just a little wild.

"Billy and I have a good mother and son relationship. He's crazy about me and I'm crazy
about him. When Billy said that he had offered me to the band, I said, 'Oh, Billy!' But I really do like them, and I would like to help Billy win the contest."

I was done with the interviews, and I knew it was time to sit down and write this story. First I went outside and took a long walk. Usually that helps to clear my head. For some reason this time it didn't seem to work.

[From the *Denver Post*, Apr. 28, 1985]
SEX VIOLENCE AND ROCK N' ROLL. YOUNG FANS CAN SEE IT ALL
(By Barbara Jaeger)

On a recent Saturday night in Passaic, N.J., rock star Billy Idol stood at the edge of the Capitol Theater   stage and encouraged two young girls to fondle him.

A couple of weeks before, at the Brendan Byrne Arena in East Rutherford, Vince Neil, lead singer of the heavymetal group *Mötley Crüe*, peppered his between song patter with sexual vulgarities and a description of the group's erotic encounters with groupies. ("We like the fat ones best," boasted Neil, "because they'll do anything.") Many of the 13,000 fans in the audience were no more than 11 or 12 years old and had been ferried to the arena by their parents.

Every day on cable television's MTV, children as young as 5 regularly watch women in chains and people being tortured and shot.

Rock 'n' roll has always been a counterculture art form, emphasizing sex and rebellion against authority. Recently, what had been merely suggestive has turned cruel and vicious, and, possibly, dangerous.

"Teenagers have not fused the idea of love and sex," says psychologist and nationally syndicated columnist Dr. Joyce Brothers, "so when you teach them that violence and sex are related, it's extremely dangerous for their future behavior."

That the music industry sees sex and violence as a marketable commodity is evidenced by a recent press release sent to pop music writers by Elektra Asylum Records. The promotional material described the latest album from *Mötley Crüe* as "dripping with impure and adulterated lust. . ."

The release began by quoting the group's bass player, Nikki Sixx: "We're the American youth. And youth is about sex, drugs, pizza, and more sex. We're intellectuals on a crotch level."

The executives at Elektra Asylum, a division of Warner Communications, refused to comment on why the company would publicize the group in this manner.

Mötley Crüe is by no means an exception. At Idol's Passaic performance, the 28 year old British rocker wore tight, black leather pants, a sleeveless black and red shirt that looked as if it had gone through a paper shredder, a studded black leather gauntlet and an Iron Cross.

When his fist wasn't raised in the air, it was groping his crotch. At one point, he writhed on the floor, a microphone shoved down the front of his pants, while two girls—who looked no older than 16—bent over him These kinds of performances are no longer restricted to concert halls and theaters . They are now being piped into homes daily.

Because of the seductiveness of the tube, in the same way that I view Sesame Street to be seductive in a positive way, I view some of the music videos in a negative way," says disc jockey Pete Fornatale, a 15 year veteran at New York rock radio station WNEW FM. "One is teaching them their ABCs and 1, 2, 3s and the other is teaching them to bring knives to concerts and to defile as many women as they can in the shortest time possible."

MTV, the 24 hour rock music channel, has come under heavy fire by such groups as Women Against Pornography and the National Coalition on Television Violence. In a recent report, the NCTV said more than half the videos on MTV feature violence, or strongly suggest violence.

Among the videos cited by the NCTV are Michael Jackson's "Thriller" ("features a very appealing young hero having fun terrorizing his girlfriend with horror violence'), the *Rolling Stones'* "Undercover of the Night" ("features intense automatic weapons violence…including a violent lawless execution") and Idol's "Dancing With Myself' ("filmed by the producer of *The Texas Chainsaw Massacre*, has a naked woman struggling in chains behind a translucent sheet").

Says Dr. Thomas Radecki, NCTV chairman and a psychiatrist on the staff of the University of Illinois School of Medicine: "The message is that violence is normal and OK, that hostile sexual relations between men and women are common and acceptable, that heroes actively engage in torture and murder of others for fun."

In response, the management of MTV has issued the following statement: "MTV is not pro violent and we're not advocating violence. And at this point in time, it's not an issue we're willing to debate in the press."

In fairness to the cable channel, its management has rejected videos because of violence and nudity (a scene from the *Stones'* "She Was Hot" was deemed as going "beyond the bounds of good taste," although an edited version is now airing), and MTV has pulled other videos after a public outcry (*Van Halen's* "(Oh) Pretty Woman," which featured, among other things, bondage and fondling).

Evelina Kane, a member of Women Against Pornography, says the most disturbing aspect of rock videos is the amount of violence directed toward women. "The message of most videos is about sex and sex roles and the perpetuation of the myth of men as active and women as passive," Kane says. "With the prominence of scanty costumes and the dominance of men, what's being reintroduced is the idea of women as either good girls or whores."

Idol, according to his publicist, Ellen Golden, says critics of his videos are "missing their points'. He says the theme of "Dancing With Myself" is the struggle for freedom and the chained woman represents Oktobriana, a symbol of the struggle for liberation in the Russian Revolution. (On his left arm, Idol sports a tattoo of Oktobriana.) And in "White Wedding," when he jams a wedding band on his bride's finger, drawing blood in the process, Idol says, he is illustrating men's cruelty to women.

Violence and sex also are prevalent—and explicit—in many of today's rock lyrics. Kiss' latest album is "Lick It Up." In addition to the title track, it includes such songs as "Not for the Innocent," "Young and Wasted" and "Gimme More".

Album covers today routinely feature women in bondage ("Vices" by *Waysted* depicts a woman in handcuffs and chains), bizarre creaturs   (Ozzy Osbourne as a werewolf on "Bark at the Moon") and violence (the *Scorpions'* "Blackout" shows a man in a straitjacket with forks stuck in his eyes).

Of course, the rock world has always generated its share of
controversy. Elvis Presley's pelvic gyrations were deemed
so suggestive that when he appeared on "The Ed Sullivan
Show" in 1956, the cameramen were ordered to shoot him
from the waist up. When the *Rolling Stones* released "(I
Can't Get No) Satisfaction" in 1965, the song was banned by
numerous radio stations because of its suggestive lyrics.
When the Stones appeared on "Sullivan," censors changed
the lyrics of "Let's Spend the Night Together" to "Let's
spend some time together."

Some industry leaders laugh at criticism of lyrics and
behavior , saying that rock's essence is the wild and
outrageous. "All the theatrical trappings—the tight
costumes, the pyrotechnics, the actions—are just good show
business," said veteran concert promoter Ron Delsener, who
presents concerts at the Meadowlands Sports Complex in
East Rutherford, N.J.

Others, like rock critic and author Dave Marsh, liken the
actions of organizations such as NCTV to a witch hunt. "I
have no problem with violence when it is used for a
purpose," says Marsh. "For example, in the 'Beat It' video
(in which Michael Jackson unites two warring gangs
through dance), the violence is used to promote racial
harmoney .

But can the viewing audience of MTV and other
video outlets—which includes children as young as 5—and
teenage concertgoers differentiate between violence used
for a dramatic purpose and violence used strictly for
exploitation?

No, say Dr. Gladys Halvorsen, a Tenafly, N.J., child and
adolescent psychiatrist, and Vincent Androsiglio, a family
therapist with a practice in Teaneck, N.J.

"What young people are seeing and hearing is a distortion
of what life is all about," Halvorsen says. "And this
distortion can have damaging effects. At this
impressionable age, young people need strong role models,
and they're not getting them.

"Exposure to such things can result in an entire range of
damaging possibilities from emotional effects to lethal

ones, which could lead them to act in the same say,"
Halvorsen adds.

The amount of damage caused by viewing destructive
behavior   has been disputed since the U.S. surgeon general
released a report on television violence in 1972. The report
found short term consequences but was sketchy on long
term effects. The information was updated in 1982 by the
National Institute of Mental Health, which found that
"television violence is as strongly correlated with
aggressive behavior   as any behavioral   variable that
has been measured."

 The television industry disputed these findings. NBC
countered with a report of its own that found "no evidence
of a causal connection between television violence and the
development of aggressive behavior   patterns among
children and adolescents."

WAPs Kane cites the results of a recent study by Edward
Donnerstein, a psychologist and found that men became
desensitized to violence against women after watching such
sexually violent films as "Vice Squad" and "Texas Chainsaw
Massacre."

Not all rock groups should be condemned for the violence
and sexual behavior   touted by some. Neither "Brass in
Pocket" nor "The Kid"   two videos from the Pretenders
 is violent. Yet the band, fronted by Chrissie Hynde, is
selling out during its current cross country tour.
One of the biggest success stories last year was written by
the politically conscious Irish band *U2* Led by charismatic
lead singer Bono, the group scored big with the album
"War," sold out dates throughut   the country.

[From the *Voice*, June 18, 1985]
WHITE NOISE -- HOW HEAVY METAL RULES
(By Deborah Frost)

It's Friday night at *L'Amour, Rock Capital* of Brooklyn
(well, that's what it says on the awning). The smell is smoke
and damp, black lipstick and black leather. God   and
maybe the fire marshal—knows how many bodies are packed
shag to shag, Bud to Bud, in front of the oversized video
screen and overworked P.A. Fists jump, jab, and pump as the

crowd screams the catchphrases to songs you probably won't hear on contemporary hit radio: "YOU CAN'T STOP IT, YOU JUST CAN'T STOP IT, YOU CANT STOP ROCK & ROLL! PLAY DIRTY! BALLS TO THE. WALL! SHOUT AT THE DEVIL! I'M AN ANIMAL, I FUCK LIKE A BEAST! HEAVY METAL, HEAVY DAYS!"

Judging by the photo buttoms , pins, and cloth logo patches splattered liberally across sleeves and bosoms, just about everybody here loves Ozzy Osbourne, *Van Halen, AC/DC, Irn Maiden*, and *Mötley Crüe*. Also popular are chains, dog collars, and the latest in welcome to my nightmare gear— spiked gauntlets whose only purpose is give a nice whaap to anyone who inadvertently gets too close.

Onstage, the band's got problems. Then again, offstage, this band has problems. Its name is *Saxon*, and their resemblance to the fictional *Spinal Tap* is not entirely coincidental. *Spinal Tap's* creators could hardly have imagined that the balding, inept bunch they parodied so perfectly would have become a commercial prospect. Halfway through *Saxon's* first song, just as the zucchini shaped bulge in frontman Biff Byford's white tights begins to wilt noticably , "The Power and the Glory" becomes "The Power Failure" *and L'Amour, Rock Capital* of Brooklyn, is plunged into darkness. "Oh, this is nothing," says Saxon's publicist. "In San Francisco, they blew out two city blocks!"

The technical difficulties are eventually conquered, enabling any interested person to discover that the solos sound the same whether the guitar player is using his fingers or bouncing the instrument off his head. There is also an endless drum solo, a couple of feeble swipes at the cymbals with flaming drumsticks, fireworks, and between song patter during which Byford addresses the audience as "you fuckers" and "you rabble" and raises such weighty subjects as big tits.

The crowd reaction might be summed up by the exuberant whoop of one boy. "Jesus, I'm psyched!" he shouts, as he and his buddies head out after the last encore, unzip their flies, and take long leaks outside the door.

"It is now 1976" mourned Lester Bangs in *The Rolling Stone Illustrated History of Rock and Roll*, "and heavy metal seems already to belong to history."

It is now 1985, and heavy metal is bigger and more profitable than ever. Despite the predictions of critics, trendsetters, and parents everywhere, heavy metal refused to roll over and die. Around the world—in London, Paris, L.A., Brooklyn—it's ALIVE! And it's still rock's crudest, grossest extreme. Which, of course, has just about everything to do with its appeal.

But no matter whether it's mass appeal (like *Van Halen*) or limited appeal (like *Mercyful Fate, Exciter*) what distinguishes new metal from old metal (like *Led Zeppelin*) is its debt to punk. True, punk failed to reach a mass audience, but thanks to its influence new metal is faster and shorter and played with more conviction than old. To paraphrase *Def Leppard's* Joe Elliot, punk failed not only because it was heavy metal with non soloing guitarists, but because it was heavy metal without heavy sex. Although other ever popular topics for metal rumination are power, death, revenge, and madness, most male, teenagers—still metal's prime audience—are not particularly interested in any product that does not offer the promise of getting laid, or at least clues of to how to go about it.

One of the oddities of heavy metal is how many bands dress up a   women's clothes   in high heels, fishnet, heavy makeup, and dyed long hair—to deliver their abuse. What's even odder is the number of girls who line up to take it. Ten years ago, females were scarce at most heavy metal shows. Now, even the most stereotypically "macho" bands—like *Judas Priest*—are drawing more sexually integrated crowds. And though metal has yet to produce a major female star, the few women in the genre—Lita Ford, *Rock Goddess, Girlschool*—are accepted as a matter of fact, something that would have been unthinkable a decade ago, when women with greater gifts (Birtha) faced far more audience hostility.

"Heavy metal is a very necessary kind of music in terms of emotional needs for a certain group," says *Mötley Crüe/ Twisted Sister* producer Tom Werman, an MBA from Columbia who sold soap for Proctor & Gamble before becoming an A&R man and producer whose acts have sold a total of 100 million records.

Not only have the musical alternatives to metal become more mechanized, they've become more respectable. Rock has moved

more and more into the mainstream, turning into TV
soundtracks and advertising jingles. Perhaps that's why
what heavy metal brings back to rock & roll now has never
seemed so sorely missed or so desperately needed—and that
is: hot blood [.

Heavy metal is still hard, fast, deep dark, and dirty. The
lyrics of some of the most successful hearvy acts—Ozzy
Osbourne and *Iron Maiden,* for instance may be largely
unintelligible, buried in a murky mix. But along with the
horror movie props, salutes, Satanic symbolism, they give the
fan the sense of belonging to a secret society, complete with
codes and initiation rites—all for the price of a concert
ticket.

Heavy metal bands invariably face the dilemma of cleaning
up their acts and their sound to the tightrope between
commercial success and "selling out" gracefully. Eddie Van
Halen (the heavy guitar hero of the generation) helped
Michael Jackson beat it to good clean crossover
superstardom. But a *Van Halen* show, unlike the
Jacksons' Victory tour, is still not a family picnic. And
you probably won't find the Social Register groupies,
who've helped turn the Stones into international
embarrassments, hanging out in Ozzy's or *Motorhead's*
dressing room. And there're going to have to be several
changes of the guard before *Mötley Crüe's* Nikki Sixx is
invited to tea in the Rose Garden.

"A kid puts on a *Judas Priest* or an *Iron Maiden* or a
Motorhead shirt and it makes a statement," says Cliff
Burnstein who used to manage *AC/DC* and now handles *Def
Leppard, Armoured Saint, Kokken* [*Dokken* , and *Metallica.*
"Hall and Oates don't make a statement."
So what statement is the kid making? He's telling society
where he stands—outsie   of it. He's telling the adult
world to fuck off.

Whatever heavy metal means to the kids who buy it today, it
means something else to the men who sell it. Even if heavy
metal never received much respect from critics or anyone
else, it's been a staple of the record industry since the
dawn of *Led Zeppelin* and *Black Sabbath.*

Throughout the '70s, for example, Deep Purple was Warner
Bros.' best selling band—a fact that convinced Bill Aucoin

to quit his day job in 1978 to manage *Kiss*, then considered a joke on the Max's/Mercer circuit ruled by the New York Dolls. Despite ups, downs, and changes of eyeliner, *Kiss* subsequently sold more than 50 million records and set the precedent for current bands like *Twisted Sister* and *Mötley Crüe*, not only in makeup but, perhaps more important, in merchandising. And well into the '80s long after the group's actual demise, *Led Zeppelin*— and eventually anything that sounded remotely like them (i.e., *AC/DC*) - not only continued to sell records but were constantly in demand on radio request lines.

As Jerry Jaffe, vice president of A&R at Phonogram, explains, heavy metal fans remain more loyal than any other record buyers. 'This is the only genre," he says, "with big catalogue between albums. You don't see that in pop acts. With pop acts, when the life of a particular Linda Ronstadt album is over, it drops to nothing. And then the next album comes out and starts selling again. But the catalogue on hard rock is phenomenal. We were selling about 10,000 albums a week of Blackout by the *scorpions* [*The Scorpions* even when it was four years old."

That loyalty comes from a band's persistent contact with its audience. *The Scorpions*, for instance, have been touring steadily since 1978, when they debuted at the bottom of a Ted Nugent/*Aerosmith* bill. They were following the traditional route for breaking heavy metal bands. The idea was to keep them on the road, building their followings until they had the reputation or the hit record that would turn them into headliners and/or stars.

What accelerated and revolutionized the process was MTV. Without it, it's possible that the current heavy metal boom might have happened anyway, but it probably wouldn't have been so popular or so lucrative. "A lot of people," says Tom Werman, "were introduced to heavy metal who didn't really know about it before."

Cliff Burstein points to a *Forbes* market research study that directly connects the surge of MTV watching and record sales with the bottoming out of the video game business. Burnstein feels that heavy metal made such an impression on video because "these groups, their raison d'être almost, is to play live. On the videos, they have some excitement.'

Def Leppard created enough excitement   thanks to several
hit singles and a somewhat softer, more melodic approach -
to sell more than six million copies of their third album,
Pyromania. Although it couldn't compete with Michael
Jackson's 40 million Thrillers (what could?), it was the
second largest selling album of 1983. As a result, the band's
earlier albums began selling briskly, too. *Quiet Riot's* 1984
debut LP sold 4.5 million copies. No surprise that record
executives have been more impressed by *Quiet Riot* than
anyone else: their debut cost only $30,000 to make. Although
more industry spokespeople quickly point out that the cost
of the average heavy metal record is closer to $125,000
(which usually includes a hefty percentage to an
experienced producer and engineer to maintain order in the
studio and make the product hit tight), the potential profit
margin is still great.

MTV had another, perhaps more disturbing, effect. "I think
the androgynous nature of so many of the 'new music' acts
forced a polarization of sexuality that was even more
graphically brought into focus by the rise of MTV,"
explains Jerry Jaffe. "So basically you had a much more
macho image present in the music. *Van Halen* is the ultimate
fantasy for all these guys. Don't forget, most of this genre
of music—the way that it is programmed for radio and MTV,
you have to understand, is the lowest common denominator
entertainment. It's bread and circuses for the common people.
Record companies are trying to make money. In the same way
that Porky's made money, a record company can make money
on *Mötley Crüe*."
Hello Boston? Do you motherfuckers like to drink alcohol?
Do you motherfuckers like to eat pussy? Do you know why
our fuckin' hearts are broken tonight, Boston? Because we
can't eat all that Boston pussy tonight. Hello Boston! Do
you motherfuckers like to drink alcohol? Do you
motherfuckers like to eat pussy? Hello Boston! Do you
motherfu . . .

It's Tuesday maybe, but it's not Boston. It's somewhere in
the flashfire warning area way above Malibu, where a tape
of a *Mötley Crüe* show has just blown out the monitor system
of a rustic studio tucked into the dry brush up in the
hills. The three fourths of *Mötley Crüe* present are not
really interested in mixing a performance tape for an
upcoming live broadcast. That's partly because the tape
exposes the bum notes and painful realities you don't hear

on their brilliantly produced second album, Shout at the Devil, or see in their impeccably directed videos, where they're draped in $20,000 worth of studded leather costumes, several layers of elaborate makeup, and hordes of hired women.

Bass player Nikki Sixx's day began at the Hyatt on Sunset with an oath never to drink again, an Alka Seltzer, and a shot of Jack Daniel's. He keeps the Jack in his black 1984 Stingray along with a hairbrush and a giant economy size can of Flex Net.

Nikki and drummer Tommy Lee say they always like to keep their hair looking cool and their Corvettes washed so they can get laid. Like last night. They weren't actually planning to stay at the Hyatt, that's just the way things turned out. Back in the old days, it used to be nicknamed the Riot House and lots of bands (who liked to do the same shit the *Crüe* likes to do now) used to stay there. But these days, most rock and rollers stay at the Marquis down farther on Sunset, where no one'd blink if they say   Nikki like he was last night on the little couch in front of the elevator on their manager's floor sorta like a dead cockroach, with his feet up in the air and Tommy yelling, "C'mon man, we're never gonna get laid if you keep lying there!"

But, oh that was nothing compared to the time (where was it?) when guitarist Mick Mars got arrested for indecent exposure, but it was really a case of mistaken identity 'cause it was Tommy who was running down the hall in his party pants   they're sorta like a leather G string.

He has 'em in leopard, too. Only the senile security guard, the guy was like 70 years old, man, just saw bare cheeks and Revlon Blue/Black hair and went into the men's room on the floor, and there was Mick, just talkin' to a chick, man. And the next thing Mick knew he was in handcuffs, going to spend the night in jail. He got bailed out, the hotel apologized, and all charges were dropped. The thing was mishandled terribly, man.

But everyone in this band's been in jail a million times. It's a joke. Like the story that got out about Vince beating up a girl on Halloween? That was no girl, that was Tommy, man! Who remembers what it was about? You get a little liquor in you and you throw a few punches and Tommy broke Vince's nose. And then the cops came and beat up Vince so bad the faggots in the cell wouldn't even look at him.

Okay, so, yeah, well, last night…Ever since he rolled some chick's 240Z off the Ventura Freeway and practically killed himself (but so what? The band would've been HUGE), his little sister Athena, her old boyfriend, and the chick who was stupid enough to let him drive her car in the first place. Tommy's gotten a little wiser about driving when he's twisted. Even if Traffic School and A.A., like they made him go to, is a joke, man!

Anyway, lots of times Tommy just goes back to Nikki's place in Coldwater Canyon and bones some chick on the living room floor. But last night when their manager saw the condition they were in when they came back from the Seventh Veil, or maybe it was the Bodyshop, with a couple of chicks who work there…see, well, the exact chain of events is a little hard to remember. That's what happens when you get a couple mudslides in you. If you don't know what they are, maybe that's cause in New York they're called screaming orgasms. They're kahlua and run   and vodka and who knows what else but after maybe two of 'em, you start seeing God.

Anyway, they were drinking mudslides at the Hyatt and then when they started biting people, their manager took away the keys to their 'vettes and made them stay in the hotel. Biting? Oh, that's just a little roll, a new hot tip, they got into on the road after they got tired of BB guns which they got into after whatever else they were doing in the way of trashing rooms got kinda old. You know what happens when you shoot up a motel room with BBs, don't you? The problem isn't just replacing the mirrors and all the stuff from room service that you used for target practice, it's that all those little pellets get really stuck in the walls and you have to replace the wallpaper and that could be at least $8000 you could really spend a lot better on lights or something that's gonna make the '85 show fuckin' incredible, man.

Vince says all of the touring in the past year, has definitely made them way more professional. Instead of trashing a motel wall (well, sometimes they don't always give you connecting rooms so you just have to make them), now they just rip up somethin'. Or bite somebody. But don't worry. They only bite people they like.

Last night that included the waitress and their manager.
He's used to it, even if he is black and blue. He's gone to
emergency rooms so often now for tetanus shots it's gotten
to be as ordinary as brushing his teeth. Yeah, you have to
get a tetanus shot if the skin gets broken. Human bites are
worse than an animal's because of the bacteria in the
saliva. Their road manager's read up all about it. He sort
of had to. Man—in where was it? Evansville of someplace—
it was really wild. They pulled into the hospital with so
many emergencies, the fuckin' attendants didn't know who to
treat first. There was one rash, a couple of claps, and
human bites. So they just looked at this truckload and said,
okay, human bites, right this way.

The clap? Oh, that was, uh, the road crew. They're all sex
gods, too. In fact, they try out the girls before they ever
get to the band. This band has a really efficient road
manager, he really codes the backstage passes well. See, the
girls that have a patch with a slash on it, they've already
been with the road crew to get that pass. If it's a slash or
PSP, pre show pussy, that means she got that pass before the
show and the band knows to stay away from her. What would
you have to do to get that pass? Oh, probably perform some
spectacular feat in the back of the bus. Like taking on
three fourths of the road crew. If one guy gets a girl, he's
not gonna give her a pass. He's gonna have him and his
buddy back there bring on the lighting guys. Just like
everyone gets a shot at it. You find these girls that will
do just anything to get backstage. They're troupers, man.
You've never seen some girls take so much. These girls'll do
anything, man. Ask 'em to bark, they'll bark. Where do you
find them? You can find them just about anywhere. Arf!

What was really funny was the way every girl who got on
the bus had to leave a little something behind. By the end
of the tour, the bus was entirely decorated with underwear.
But they had to throw it all away somewhere before L.A.—
the whole bus fuckin' reeked.
What Nikki would rather be doing right now is get into some
serious flesh, that's what he calls it. Instead, he's waiting
for Vince to record over the worst mistakes on songs Nikki's
so sick of he says he wishes he'd never written them, like
"Merry Go Round." That's about a mental institution. Nikki
says he has a half sister who's spent her life in one, but

that's not why he's sick of the song. It's just he's learned something about hooks since he wrote it, and he realizes now it doesn't have too many.

There are these two chicks who work at one of the places on the Strip, and maybe after they're finished dancing, he and Tommy can persuade them to go back to Nikki's or some place. Tommy says he'd spend his last dollar (Nikki's down to $21.40 himself; his new instant teller card hasn't helped his cash flow any) to pay those girls to make love to one another. After you get off the road, doin' shows every night and shit, it's just nice to be able to sit back and have someone else entertain you for a change.

Nikki leafs through *Billboard.* He's not too interested in where Shout at the Devil is on the charts. Or their first album, Too Fast for Love, which they recorded on their own, before connecting with a real producer and a real manager whose family's oil wells helped pay for the $20,000 costumes, fireworks, and photos that all helped contribute to the mystique and popularity of a band with *Kiss* like makeup, a Blue Oyster Cultish logo, and whose singer and guitarist sounded a lot like *Aerosmith's* bands which previously captured the imaginations and allowances of fans the same age as *Mötley Crüe.*

Nikki turns the page to an ad for Tina Turner, studies it and for a moment, seems lost, deep in thought.

"I've never fucked a black chick," he says.

It's Thursday at the Marquee in London. The smell is smoke and pints sloshed on the floor. Oooh, there's *Hanoi Rocks!* And *Girls chool* with their new guitar player from Australia! Rock Goddess with their dad the manager, and ex Teddy boy in drainpipe trousers who taught them how to play! Neil from *Whitesnake!* And a guy who's been jamming with Jimmy Page! That's the audience.

Lita Ford is onstage. She's made a tremendous improvement since her first album. At least she's gotten rid of a costume that looked like it was pieced together from raids on Cher and Big Bird. Now she's wearing the same black Lita Ford T shirt anyone can buy out front by the bar. Her bass player has a swastika magic markered on his arm. He sometimes like to draw them in lipstick, too, on backstage mirrors. Yeah,

Hitler's sort of happening again. Ozzy Osbourne, the godfather of heavy metal, has been going onstage with a little mustache and such a great jodhpur and boots getup, you'd almost think it was the Fuhrer himself.

Back at the Marquee, there's only one black person in the crowd. He's got close cropped hair, long pointed sideburns, and a dirty sports jacket. He is rocking back and forth, back and forth, bending double to his knees, locked in spasms of silent laughter, relishing some cosmic joke to which only he knows the punchline. Lita kicks into a selection of songs from her recent album: "Lady Killer," "Dressed To Kill," "Hit and Run." Inspired, perhaps, he reaches inside his jacket and starts to pull out something dull, metallic. Later the bouncers are full of assurances that it was only a starter's pistol.

Jerry Jaffe sees heavy metal as "just another form of the pop music machine that is here with us right now. It doesn't mean more or less than those old bubblegum acts. Except the image is a little more striking. Maybe because it can be exploited a little easier through videos. But basically it's just another phase in the record industry."

Cliff Burnstein, however, says the longevity of a heavy metal band is usually quite long, as much as 12 to 15 years. He cites Rush, originally a power trio who released their first record independently and have developed a progressive individual brand of "art metal" whose audience is faithful enough to fill 20,000 seaters like Madison Square Garden regardless of the success of a particular album.

A new band gets only a couple of shots, according to Jaffe. "You don't have to go so much by airplay. You can see how much they're improving in what a promoter will pay for them and the sales, because that really is the bottom line. If a new act sells 30,000 albums, I pick up the option, and the next one sells 75,000, we would be $250,000 in the hole. But because I see they've doubled their audience, I might go for a third album."

But because, as Jaffe suggest , this is the only genre where a band can build a substantial audience by touring, record companies have reinstituted a practice from pre slumpdays —tour support. It's necessary, because despite the high ticket prices (*Iron Maiden*, for example, charged $17.50 at

Radio City), the "special guests" (i.e., opening acts) may receive only $4000 to $5000. "A very special guest," according to Jaffe, may make as much as $7500. "An opening act without a big record yet has to settle—with a very benevolent headliner—for $1500."

Some of the expenses of touring can be offset by merchandise advances. As Cliff Burnstein explains, heavy metal bands sell far more merchandise (in some cases, like *Motorhead's*, they may sell more T shirts than records) than such successful pop acts as Hall and Oates, for example, who've had more top 40 hits than just about all of the heavy metal bands put together. Bands no longer assume any risk for shirts, bandanas, party hats, and assorted favors kids may not go far. Merchandising was once an afterthought, often turned out by the people who did custom work for record companies. Now there are at least three major firms—Brockum, Great Southern, and Winterland—actively competing for the rights to manufacture and sell rock merchandise. Both the companies and the bands are reluctant to disclose their merchandise revenues - and unlike the record business, which has the RIAA to certify sales, organization that monitors which T shirsts   go gold or platinum. Many have.

Jaffe says some bands are getting as much as $1 million advances for T shirts and assorted merchandise. Other sources say the figure, for an established heavy metal band, is $250,000. A new band without strong hype or a strong gimmick may get $25,000. The successful heavy metal band will sell a T shirt (or football jersey) for $10 to $14 to at least 50 per cent   of the audience. The merchandising companies usually travel with their own trucks and crews, arrange for licenses and sales tax, and make their own deals with the hall. In some cases, halls may take as much as 40 per cent, but if the band has a good deal with the merchandiser, the hall's percentage doesn't affect their cut. Many bands, says Jaffe, may make 50 per cent of their income from merchandise. Not unusual was one band, without a current record out, who returned home from a 83 date tour in medium sized (average audience under 10,000) halls with $350,000 in T shirt and novelty proceeds.

It's sometime in California. After a while the days all run together and don't make too much difference. *Mötley Crüe* are attempting to practice in a rehearsal room in

Hollywood.

Oh, I want to bone Trace right *now*, says Mick Mars to one of
the roadies, clenching his fists and making a little sort of
forward thrust as if he really means it. He is wearing red
women's spindly high heeled boots and black eyeliner,
without which he looks a lot like Don Rickles in a Morticia
Addams wig. There is no trace of any Trace, but there are
two girls the roadies found hanging around the parking lot
when they went out for a couple of six packs. They work at
an Arby's across the way, which is why the road manager
insists they must be 16, even though they look at least two
years younger. One has braces on her teeth. Both giggle a
lot. Everybody knows you have to be 16 to work at Arby's,
that's what the road manager says. These guys have heads
on their shoulders, you know. Even on the road they don't
go around pulling 14 year old chicks. We have some very
strict rules about that. What if some cop came back to the
bus and took a look at what was going on?

And there are other distractions - a box of bondage boots
and T shirts from Detroit. Some chick sent them to the New
York office. Remember Red from Detroit?
Yeah, Red. Didn't Vince bone her? I only boned her 'cause
she was buggin' me, then she wouldn't leave, says Vince.

Lead singer Vince Neil doesn't stick around too long
himself. Rehearsals take too much out of his voice. Anyway,
this is supposed to be a "creative rehearsal" to work out
new material. The only thing that really gets worked out is
a cover of the old Mountain hit "Mississippi Queen." They go
through two other songs. "Raise Your Hand to Rock" sounds
like a cross between BTO's "Ain't Seen Nothin' Yet" (melody)
and "Down in the Valley, Valley So Low" (guitar part), but
maybe it'll come together when their producers get hold of
it. Nikki is working on something else, the gist of which is
that even presidents and heads of state can be lonely.
For maybe 10 minutes, Nikki—whose mother has been married
five or six times, he forgets, which is why he left home at
13 in the first place, he says—isn't so lonely. He invites
the little girl with braces to go into the strange closet.
Meanwhile, Tommy entertains the studio by bending over and
letting it all hang out of his party   pantless gray
sweat shorts. When Nikki comes out of the closet, he takes a
stroll over to the soundstage around the corner where *WASP*,
the latest heavies from L.A., are doing a video for their
metal underground hit "(Animal) Fuck Like a Beast." Only

on the soundtrack they are miming vigorously to it's "(Animal) Bleep like a Beast."

The three front guys in WASP look like they're about seven feet tall, even without their platform stilts. Leather shorts, latex pants, and fashion accessories like over the shoulder exhaust pipes and beneath the crotch rotary blades add to the effect. Skulls and torches glow and burn on the walls behind them.

"Smoke it up! Smoke it up!" shouts the director. Gray , billowing smoke clouds offer a sneak preview of hell as cameraman on a crane moves in on the lead creature's grimace.

"You know what's wrong with those guys?" asks Nikki, walking off the sound stage shaking his Revlon Blue/Black head sadly. "They have no sense of humor. "

In   December 8, 6:38 p.m., a 1972 Pantera driven by *Mötley Crüe's* lead singer Vince Neil skidded into a lane of oncoming traffic in Redondo Beach, hitting a Volkswagen containing a 20 year old man and an 18 year old woman. Both suffered severe injuries. Neil's passenger, Hanoi Rocks drummer Nicholas Dingley, was pronounced dead en route to the hospital. Neil, who was not hurt in the accident, was arrested on charges of drunken driving and vehicular homicide. He is currently free on $2500 bail.

ATTACHMENT (A)
PORNOGRAPHY IN ROCK MUSIC

* *Judas Priest*
DEPENDERS OF THE FAITH
(2 million copies sold)

"Eat Me Alive"

Sounds like an animal panting to the beat
Groan in the pleasure zone, gasping from the heat.
Gut wrenching frenzy that destroys every joint
I'm gonna force you at gun point

To eat me alive...squealing in passion as the rod steel injects.

* *Motley Crue*
TOO FAST FOR LOVE

"Live Wire"
(currently have a song on the charts)

I'll either break her face or take down her legs..
Get my ways at will
Go for the throat, never let loose
Going in for the kill...

["]Piece of Your Action"

Tight action, Rear tract1on
So hot you really blow me away.
Fast moving, wet and ready
Time is right so hang on tight.
Live wire, night prowler
Lay back and take me inside.
I want a piece of your action...

SHOUT AT THE DEVIL
(double platinum album)
"Too Young to Fall in Love"

Not a woman, but a whore.
I can taste the hate.
Well, now I a killing you...
Watch your face turning blue...

"Bastard"

Out go the lights
In goes my knife
Pull out his life
Consider that bastard dead.
Make it quick
Blow off his head...

"There's so much good pussy in Alburquerque! The only thing wrong is that I can't eat it all tonight!"—From *Hit Parader* —Vince Neil to a concert crowd...

- *Quiet Riot*

METAL HEALTH
(over 5 million copies sold)

"Let's Get Crazy"

Lookin for some action
Wanna mean machine
Gettin' hot and nasty
Climbing in between
I'm gonna find a mamma
That makes me feel alright
Wanna kiss your lips
Not the ones on your face.

- Prince

DIRTY MIND
"Sister"

I was only 16,
But I guess that's no excuse.
My sister was 32
Lovely and lose .
My sister never made love to anyone but me.
Incest is everything it's said to be.

PURPLE RAIN
(over 9 million sold)
"Darling Nikki"

I knew a girl named Nikki
I guess you could say she was a sex fiend.
I met her in a hotel lobby masturbating with a magazine.

Prince's stage show included a guitar that "ejaculated" water
into the crowd after he simulated masturbation with it..

- *AC/DC*

"Let Me Put My Love Into You"
Don't you stuggle
Don't you fight
Let me put my love into you
Let me cut your cake with my knife.

- *Wrathchild*

STAKK ATAKK

"Trash Queen"

There's a lady out on the street
So hungry, looking for meat...
For a price she'll spread her legs
She's a trash queen
What do you do for pain or pleasure?
(woman panting and groaning in the background)

"Sweet Surrender"

I lick my lips and make advances
You lay on down and let me in
But you can't fight
You got no chance.
I'll tame you down and rub my cream in...
Shock me
Right in between my legs.
Rock me...
Oh you're so tight.
Oh wham Bam
Thank you ma'am.

- *Twisted Sister* - Atlantic Records

"We acted out a scene in a middle American home with a strict father who yells and screams at his son for listening to roll   and roll. He lays a tirade on his son and the last line is 'what do you want to do with your life?' Instead of being like a beaten dog the kid says in an exorcist-like voice, "I WANT TO ROCK!" and gets transformed into me! I change my brothers into the other band members and we proceed to destroy Daddy; Smash him with doors, pull him by the hair...(The father is pulled down the stairs by his hair... Blown out a bedroom wall...etc...)

UNDER THE BLADE
"Under the Blade"

Your hands are tied,
Your legs are strapped
You're going under the blade...
Bitch

BE MY SLAVE
"Leatherbound"

The whip is my toy
Handcuffs are your joy
You hold me down and I'm screaming for more...
When you tie me up and gag me
The way you give me pain
Give me lashes
C'mon and drag me...

• *KISS*

LICK IT UP
"Fits Like a Glove"

Ain't a cardinal sin baby
Let me in
Girl I'm gonna treat you right.
Well goodness sakes
My snake's alive and it's ready to bite...
Baby let me in.
Fits like a glove...
Think I'm gonna burst.
When I go through her...
It's like a hot knife through butter.

• *Rock Goddess*
HELL HATH NO FURY

"Hold Me Down"

Hold me down, Take me down
I want to make it with you more than anything
Let your love come inside
Be a bad boy for this bad girl
Give me heaven and I'll give you hall...

• *Venom*
"Possessed"

Look at me, Satans Child

Born of evil, thus defiled.
Brought to life through satanic birth
Come look at me and
I'll show you things that will open your eyes...
Listen to me and I'll tell you things that will sicken your mind..
I drink the vomit of the priests,
Make love with the dying whore...
Satan as my master incarnate
Hail, praise to my unholy host…

- 	*Great White*
"On Your Knees"

Kickin down your door
Gonna pull you to the floor
Taking what I choose
Never gonna lose
Gonna drive my love inside you
Gonna nail your ass to the floor...

- 	*Vanity*
VANITY 6

"Strap On Robby Baby"

Come on and stroke me.
Strap this thing tight.
If you want to glide down my hallway, it's open.
Strap yourself in and ride
I wanna glide down your carnival.

- 	*W.A.S.P.*
"Fuck Like a Beast"

I got pictures of naked ladies
Lying on my bed.
I whiff the smell of a sweet convulsion.
Thoughts are sweating inside my head.
I'm making artificial love for free...
I start to howl in heat...
I fuck like a beast...
I come steal your love.

- *Morris Day and the Time*
ICE CREAM CASTLES

"If the Kid Can't Make You Come"

I wanna get you off baby...
You can stradle   my brass

As we dance in the land of hard and soft...
If the Kid can't make you come
Nobody can...

Editor: Jay Rosen

POP LYRICS:
A Mirror and a Molder
**Sheila Davis of Society*

IN THE THIRTY-ONE YEARS since Et cetera published S.I. Hayakawa's paper "Popular Songs vs. the Facts of Life" assessing the "underlying assumptions, orientations, and implied attitudes" reflected in pop lyrics, (1) major social forces have combined to reshape the sound and the content of our songs -- the Sexual Revolution; the Women's Movement; the dominance in the recording marketplace by the creative hyphenate (the singer-songwriter-arranger-producer); and the growing "africanization" of American music. (2) If Dr. Hayakawa were listening to top-40 radio today, he would hear a radical change in both the attitudes and the language of popular songs.

For one thing, the belief in magic, miracles, and a love to last forever—manifest in so many pre-rock era songs— is expressed only occasionally in contemporary lyrics. Lionel Richie would seem to be the last bastion of romanticism, still proclaiming the viability of "Endless Love," and effecting an open-hearted vulnerability in "Truly" and "Still." Today long-term interpersonal relationships are more generally viewed as difficult, if not impossible, as in such hits as "Hard Time For Lovers" and "What's Forever For?" In spite of an occasional "we can work it out" sentiment, the overriding emotion is disillusionment, reflecting the current one-out-of-three divorce rate.

Female passivity, like commitment, is out of style. The lyrical wimp, who Hayakawa heard whining in "Can't Help Lovin' Dat Man," has been replaced with the EST-inspired assertiveness of such feminist anthems as "I Will Survive" and "It's My Turn." In fact, the top female recording stars of the mid-eighties—Cyndi Lauper, Madonna, Sheena Easton, and Tina Turner—seem to be speaking for a whole new breed of woman—bold, tough, and materialistic—("Girls Just Want to Have Fun," "Money Changes Everything," and "Material Girl")—seeking, along with equal pay, equal sexual satisfaction—with or without a partner. It was, indeed, a female singer, Cyndi Lauper, who took the subject of auto eroticism out of the closet of male album cuts and into the spotlight of single hits in "She Bop." (3) Suggestive lyrics have traditionally employed metaphor, double entendre, or the vagueness of the word it (long a stand-in for copulation) to evade the censure of blue pencils. Back in 1928 Cole Porter's "Let's Do It" was qualified by the line "Let's fall in love." By the sixties the Beatles could dispense with the hedge and get away with a more direct, if somewhat funky invitation: "Why Don't We Do It in the Road (No one will be watching us)" which, repeated endlessly, constituted the song's entire lyric. The semantics of it in contemporary songs has progressed on two levels: from something the singer is thinking about doing to something the singer is in the act of doing; and from the act of coitus in general to the act of fellatio or cunnilingus in particular as in such recent hit titles as "Do It Any You Want (But do it, do it, do it, do it)," "Do You Like It Girl," "I Like To Do It," "I Wanna Do It to You," and "Lick It Up."

Not only has explicitness displaced subtlety, and the erotic territory expanded to include masturbation and oral sex, but lyrics have even invaded the once taboo terrain of incest. Rock superstar Prince, for example, whose pornographic output includes the ode to fellatio "Head," gives the green light to familiar intimacy in "Sister": She was thirty-two and lonely, he was sixteen and innocent, and "Incest is everything it's said to be." (4)

It is apparent that we've entered the age of hard core lyrics. Dr. Hayakawa wouldn't believe his ears: For example, the endlessly repeating chorus of "Relax... when you want to come," accompanied by a synthesized orgasmic beat, filled the airways around the world in 1984 and 1985 (5); Sheena Easton, in another 1985 megahit, invited her partner to "spend the night inside my sugar walls" (6); Oscar award winner Prince, addressing Sheila E. in the duet "Erotic City" gets down to specifics, "I just want your creamy thighs/We could f—— until the dawn" (7); And just in case a listener doesn't catch the message on the stereo, it's all spelled out on the lyric sheets that accompany the albums.

The language of today's four-letter "sexplicitness" was recently deplored by Smokey Robinson, recording artist and vice president of Motown Records, as "a situation in desperate need of change." (8)

That songs speak for their time is a given. But they are more than mere mirrors of society; they are a potent force in the shaping of it. In this increasingly acoustic world, popular songs—whose attitudes and injunctions are walked to, danced to, chanted, and internalized — provide the primary "equipment for living" for America's youth. (9) The power of lyrics to persuade, and even to incite to action has long been known. In no previous decade perhaps was this power more manifest than in the sixties when the Beatles glamorized viewing the world through LSD's "kaleidoscope eyes." (10) By endorsing and thereby promoting practices that society deems illegal or immoral, pop lyrics act to accelerate the acceptance of such behavior   as the norm.

When we consider that cocaine is now peddled in the corners of our schoolyards, and that the rate of teenage pregnancy "leads nearly all other developed nations of the world," (11) might it not be worthwhile for semanticists and journalists (as well as sociologists) to give serious attention to the content of pop songs and to evaluate not only what its lyrics are saying to society, but more importantly, what they may be doing to it?

NOTES AND REFERENCES

1. Dr. Hayakawa'a paper was originally presented at the Second Conference on General Semantics, held under the auspices of Washington University and the St. Louis Chapter of the International Society for General Semantics, at St. Louis, Missouri, June 12, 1954 and published in Et cetera in Winter, 1955, Vol. XII, No. 2, pp. 83-95.
2. Henry Pleasants in Serious Music and All That Jazz (New York: Simon and Schuster, l959), p. 194, quotes British music critic Charles Keil (Urban Blues, 1966): "It is simply incontestable thar year by year, American popular music has come to sound more and more like African popular music."
3. "She Bop" written by Cyndi Lauper/Stephen S. Lunt/Gary Corbett/Rick Chertoff; © 1984 Reilla Music/Perfect Punch/Hobbler Music/Noyb Music Co.
4. 'Sister' written by Prince, © 1981 Controversy Music from the LP "Dirty Mind" on the Warner Brothers label.
5. "Relax" written by Johnson/O'Toole/Gill; © 1984 Perfect Songs/Island; recorded by the group Frankie Goes to Hollywood on ZTT/Island Records.
6. "Sugar Walls" written by Alexander Nevermind; © 1984 Tionna Music; recorded by Sheena Easton on EMI America label
7. "Erotic City" written by Prince; © 1983 Controversy Music; recorded by Prince on the "B" side of his hit single "Let's Go Crazy" on Warner Brothers label.
8. New York Times Interview with Stephen Holden, 2/15/85.
9. Kenneth Burke once described poetry as "equipment for living" whereby we are introduced vicariously to the emotions and situations which we have not yet had occasion to experience. Hayakawa characterized much of pop lyrics as poor equipment for living because they gave a "false or misleading impression of what life is likely to be" in that their ideals of love were

usually impossible ideals.

10. "Lucy in the Sky With Diamonds" written by John Lennon/Paul McCartney, © 1967 Maclen Music Ltd. The song title is widely considered to be a cryptogram for LSD. Though its writers have denied it, the lyric's content tends to substantiate the allegation.

11. New York Times editorial 3/15/85 referred to a study "just released by the Alan Guttmacher Institute."

*****

The CHAIRMAN. I am sorry. Your time has expired.

Mrs. Gore, let me begin by asking you, you have children, I understand.

Mrs. GORE. Yes, I do, four children, 12, 8, 6, and 2.

The CHAIRMAN. Does the 12-year-old buy records?

Mrs. GORE. Yes, she does, and she has been buying them since she was 7 or 8. Not a lot, but occasionally.

The CHAIRMAN. Do you have any way of knowing what is on the records that she buys?

Mrs. GORE. No, I do not have any way of knowing that.

The CHAIRMAN. There is nothing on the face of the album which would notify you if the record has pornographic material or material glorifying violence?

Mrs. GORE. No, there is nothing that would suggest that to me at this time.

The CHAIRMAN. And it would be unrealistic, wouldn't it, for a parent to go into the record store and play the record in its entirety to find out what the words are?

Mrs. GORE. Well, it is. Normally you are not allowed to open a record and play it until after you have purchased it.

The CHAIRMAN. Now, Mr. Ling, you pointed out at the beginning of your presentation that you do know of a couple of cases where kids have committed suicide while listening to rock music that advocates suicide.

Do you believe that those are rare cases of rock music influencing behavior , or do you think that it is more commonplace? In other words, do you think that this music is tasteless, but that it really does not have very much effect, or do you think that the music has some negative consequences?

Mr. LING. I think it has great effect. As one who has worked with teenagers and college students on a professional level for the last 10 years, I have watched the things that they have watched, and listened to what they have listened to. I have seen their behavior   influenced and encouraged by this music.

More importantly, sir, the problem is that the music might reflect the behavior   attitudes, values of those in the 18 or older bracket. However, when that music is listened to by 12-year-olds, 11-year-olds, and 10-year-olds, it moves from the area of being a reinforcer and an encourager into the role of educator, and many of these young children are being educated in these things before they have any kind of frame of reference to properly put it in.

The CHAIRMAN. Senator Gore.

Senator GORE. Well, Mr. Chairman, a statement was submitted for the record from Dr. Thomas Ridecki which bears upon the question about whether or not behavior   is influenced by music. If it is appropriate, I would like that to be included in the record.
The CHAIRMAN. Without objection.

Senator GORE. I would just like to reinforce a couple of statements that were made in prepared testimony. I believe, Ms. Baker, you began by saying that what you're proposing and what the group is proposing does not involve any request for Government action, is that correct?

Mrs. BAKER. That's right.

Senator GORE. When you responded to the Chairman a minute ago, you said there is no way you can tell if the record has pornographic material or material glorifying violence. In fact, some of the material has an album cover design which will indicate it, but some does not, is that correct?

Mrs. GORE. That is correct. Some of the album covers are very explicit. In fact, they look like they should be in *Playboy* or *Penthouse*, some of them, and they are in the record bins available to young children. But others, you cannot tell.

I bought the "Purple Rain" album for our 11-year-old and I did not know that "Darling Nikki" was on it, and I felt that it was inappropriate for her and her 8-and 6-year-old sisters to hear a song describing a girl masturbating in a hotel lobby with a magazine.

I had no warning. In fact, all I know was that Prince was the new creative teen idol on the scene and had just received a Grammy Award. So I would have appreciated it if I had known that before purchase.

Senator GORE. Well, I appreciate that. Thank you, Mr. Chairman.

The CHAIRMAN. Senator Rockefeller.

Senator ROCKEFELLER. It does not matter to me who answers this question, but there is a difference between the material that Mr. Ling presented and the videotapes that we viewed earlier. For example, I thought that the presentation that your particular panel made was much more to the point than the previous presentation. It was not only graphic and shocking, but there was not any question as to where to draw the line.

If something is graphic, does that cross the line? Does it have to be explicit? I understand, that 80 record companies have agreed to conform to the labeling principle.

Where should the line be drawn as to what is fantasy, which is disturbing to a parent and yet is not as dangerous as something which is graphic, explicit, and clearly dangerous to teens and pre-teens with vulnerable, unformed values?

One cannot stop everything. The companies, you are saying, are going to have to make the judgment. In your conversations with them, how do they define the line that should not be crossed?

Mrs. GORE. In our conversations with Mr. Gortikov, he has made it clear that this is a difficult area. We suggested that the industry appoint an industry-wide panel of some consumer representatives one time to discuss the set of criteria that would be used.
It would not be a list of words. It would be simply a policy statement, such as, we will be sensitive to lyrics that talk about graphic brutality toward women, violence, rape, explicit sexuality. We believe that the record companies and those individuals within those companies are best left to make those subjective decisions. There will always be areas of gray, but what we want from them is an affirmation that they will be sensitive to this concern as they individually apply a warning label within their individual companies.
We need for them to be able to get together and say, we will do this in good faith, we will go back to our individual companies, we will make those subjective decisions and judgments ourselves. That is what we are asking them to do.

Senator ROCKEFELLER. Do you think the record companies had been planning on doing this before you all approached them? I mean, this business has been going on, MTV and all the rest of it, for some time now.

I do not know how long you have been in existence, but the problem is bad and apparently getting worse. It brings to the fore the terror that exists on the part of all parents, and goes to the whole question of what it is that our children are learning and seeing that confronts us every day.

Was this simply the result of your conversations with them, that they suddenly agreed to decide to do some labeling?

Mrs. BAKER. Senator, over a year and a half ago the National PTA passed a resolution and wrote to the music industry, direct recording industry, asking them to label sexually explicit, violent, profane, or material that encouraged the use of drugs and alcohol. And that, as far as I know, got no response from the industry.

But there have been calls for this sort of thing. Some, very few but some, albums have been labeled as objectionable to some people. So there has been a little bit of this done in the industry in the past, but it has been very small. And our hope is that there would be a uniform application across the board in the recording industry to give parents and consumers warning when explicit, blatant, violent material is in the album or any music product.

Senator ROCKEFELLER. Those companies which are declining to go along with labeling, which I take it to be about 20 percent of the volume, what are they giving as reasons for not going along?

Mrs. BAKER. We have not had direct conversations with them. We have been speaking with Stanley Gortikov, who is head of the Recording Industry Association of America, and he represents the majority of companies that produce the majority of records. And so I could not speak to that.

Senator ROCKEFELLER. Is there any serious doubt with serious people to whom you have talked that there is a direct relationship between violence and disturbing tendencies and occurrences among young people and the proliferation of this type of material that we have seen this morning. Is there any serious doubt that there is not a direct relationship between those two?

Or are there some who would argue that you are simply trying to suppress first amendment rights?

Mrs. BAKER. Well, some make the point – and it is certainly true – that sex and violence pervade every level of our society today. So we would just say that music, which is a very important part of young people, young people who are forming their characters and developing their value systems, learning how to relate to the opposite sex – even what they think about sex is not defined in their minds yet.

We think that it does have an influence on these young minds. But we certainly do not blame music for the ills, all the ills that exist in the teenage population, the younger children. Senator ROCKEFELLER. Is the relationship between the escalation of the so-called MTV phenomenon and the things that we have seen this morning, and the problems that exist in the teenage population is incontrovertible in your mind?

Mrs. BAKER. Absolutely.

Senator ROCKEFELLER. Thank you, Mr. Chairman.

The CHAIRMAN. Senator Gorton?

Senator GORTON. No questions, Mr. Chairman.

The CHAIRMAN. Senator Exon?

Senator EXON. Mr. Chairman, thank you very much.

I have been around here a while and I have been through many hearings in many committees, including Armed Services on the MX missile, the strategic defense   initiative, Commerce Committee on a whole wide range of deregulation, Budget Committee with regard to the national debt and what we are going to do about cutting down expenditures of the Federal Government. This is the largest media event, both in this room and the people waiting outside, that I have ever seen.

I want to first congratulate you ladies for coming here and testifying on the concerns which you have. It seems to me that this should be voluntarily worked out without Federal legislation and without regulations.

Rock music does not appeal to me at all, but it does to my kids and it does to my grandchildren. Therefore, I agree generally with the thesis that has been brought forth here this morning, that in the arts, even though that term might be used loosely the way I view it — one of the things that I find it most difficult to do is to impose upon others what my particular beliefs are, whether those beliefs be to my children or to my grandchildren.

I do happen to believe, though, that you were correct in the thrust, I believe, of what we saw this morning, some of which was personally offensive to me and other things that were not. We all have our own individual goals, I guess, and how we view those.

I guess a key question that I would like to ask you is, if there is one thing that has come through loud and clear to me at least, it is that you do not want Federal legislation and you do not want Federal regulation, at least at this time. Is that correct?

Mrs. GORE. Yes, that is correct. We do not want legislation to remedy this problem. The problem is one that developed in the marketplace. The music industry has allowed the excesses that you saw and we believe the music industry is the entity to address those excesses. We would like them to do this voluntarily. We propose no legislative solution whatsoever.

Senator EXON. When you say legislation, do you also include the term that I use, regulation?

Mrs. GORE. Yes.

Senator EXON. Well, given that and given what I think I tried to put forth as my feelings on this, Mr. Chairman, I suppose it is nice to have these hearings and discuss these things, because I think it is a concern. But I wonder, Mr. Chairman, if we are not talking about Federal regulation and we are not talking about Federal legislation, what is the reason for these hearings in front of the Commerce Committee?
 Can anyone answer that? I did not schedule these hearings. I am glad to be here to take part in

them. But sometimes I wonder why these media events are scheduled and for what possible reason, if we are not being asked to do anything about it.

The CHAIRMAN. I think that the point is that there are problems that exist in the country that are not necessarily solved by legislation or by regulation. Fortunately, the be-all and end-all of the United States is not legislation that is enacted by Congress.
I think the point of the hearings is to provide a forum for airing what a lot of people perceive of as a real problem.

Senator EXON. Well, Mr. Chairman, that may well be and that may well be an intention of what the Congress should or should not do. As one member of the Congress, I think that we indulge in too many publicity events that are far beyond the scope of regulation and legislation, which I think is our primary purpose.

The CHAIRMAN. Senator Kasten.

Senator KASTEN. Mr. Chairman, thank you. I have no questions at this time.

The CHAIRMAN. Senator Hawkins?

Senator HAWKINS. Mrs. Baker, this is one Senator who feels that there is no absolute right to free speech. It has been my experience no one has the absolute right to yell "Fire" in a theater which is not on fire.

I believe no one has the right to poison our children with the kinds of lyrics that you have shown this committee so graphically today.

And to get back to my original tenet, I would like to know, in your experiences as mothers, where did your children first hear of the record that they asked for the money to purchase? Did they hear that on MTV? Did they see the videotape preview on MTV? Or was it on a radio station?

Mrs. BAKER. Well, my 8-year-old hears music on her clock-radio. I mean, she does not have tapes and records at this stage in her life, but she does listen to the radio.

Senator HAWKINS. And then from that she decides she would like the entire album?

Mrs. BAKER. Yes, that is right.

Senator HAWKINS. So the original exposure to this kind of — I cannot think of a good word for it, but pornography rock — would be through the public airwaves, whether it be MTV or a radio station?

Mrs. BAKER. Well, Senator, I will say this, that basically most broadcasters are very responsible. There are a few hard rock stations that play things that are pornographic, but basically your main stations do not play the worst offenders.

They will play a song on an album that will get into the top 40 and maybe have some violence or sexually explicit lyrics on the album. They will not play, generally, a song that is sexually explicit.

Times are changing, though, because recently Sheena Easton's "Sugar Walls," which is really a fairly graphic song about female genital arousal, has been on the charts and it is played 10 to 12 times a day. That is one of our concerns, that this is becoming more and more mainstream, and we feel this is the time to talk about it.

Senator HAWKINS. And if the labeling took place as you have requested, do you envision that prior to the disc jockey playing that on the radio that he would read the label?

Mrs. BAKER. Well, I will tell you. All program directors know exactly what they are playing on their records. They do not need a label to know that. That is part of their business and that is part of their job, and they know exactly what they are playing.

So I would say that it is not going to be a help for the program directors and DJ's. It is going to be a help for parents. We are the ones that need the information. Those in the business know.
Senator HAWKINS. And do you have certain stations that you do not allow your child to listen to in the home?

Mrs. BAKER. Well, it has not come to that in my house, with just an 8 year old. The big ones, you know, that is another matter. But most of them are grown and they can make their own decisions about that.

This is for the young. She is not -- the heavy metals is not something. It is others that she likes to listen to.

Senator HAWKINS. Well, it is my understanding it is no longer possible to have a successful rock album without a video; that MTV is widely viewed by children, whether their parents are home or not.

Has your group met with representatives of the TV industry?

Mrs. BAKER. Yes, we have, and MTV was originally begun to promote records. I mean, that is the whole purpose of it. And there have been some really fun things done with MTV and some really awful things done. So we have talked with them, but we will meet with them again.

Senator HAWKINS. What was their response?

Mrs. BAKER. Well, their response was that they already had standards in place. We had thought that their standards should be a little tighter for younger viewing audience . But we will be asking them to label videos that have violent or sexually explicit material in them, so that parents will know, and also to consider clustering very safe – "safe" is not a good word, but I mean harmless – videos at a time when the young audience would be viewing. So that would be our suggestion to them.

Senator HAWKINS. And when are you meeting with them again?

Mrs. BAKER. In the near future.

Senator HAWKINS. Thank you.

The CHAIRMAN. Thank you very much for being here. I know that for all of you it was not the most pleasant of experiences to read some of the lyrics in public. But it was very helpful and we appreciate your attendance.

John Denver is on the witness list. He has had to leave the hearing room for another engagement. He plans to be back. So the next witness will be Mr. Frank Zappa. Mr. Zappa, thank you very much for being with us. Please proceed.

STATEMENT OF FRANK ZAPPA, ACCOMPANIED BY LARRY STEIN, COUNSEL

Mr. ZAPPA. My name is Frank Zappa. This is my attorney Larry Stein from Los Angeles. Can you hear me?

The CHAIRMAN. If you could speak very directly and clearly into the microphone, I would appreciate it.

Mr. ZAPPA. My name is Frank Zappa. This is my attorney Larry Stein.

The statement that I prepared, that I sent you 100 copies of, is five pages long, so I have shortened it down and am going to read a condensed version of it.

Certain things have happened. I have been listening to the event in the other room and have heard some conflicting reports as to whether or not people in this committee want legislation. I understand that Mr. Hollings does from his comments. Is that correct?

The CHAIRMAN. I think you had better concentrate on your testimony, rather than asking questions.

Mr. ZAPPA. The reason I need to ask it, because I have to change something in my testimony if there is not a clearcut version of whether or not legislation is what is being discussed here.

The CHAIRMAN. Do the best you can, because I do not think anybody here can characterize

Senator Hollings' position.

Mr. ZAPPA. I will carry on with the issue, then.

Senator EXON. Mr. Chairman, I might help him out just a little bit. I might make a statement. This is one Senator that might be interested in legislation and/or regulation to some extent, recognizing the problems with the right of free expression.

I have previously expressed views that I do not believe I should be telling other people what they have to listen to. I really believe that the suggestion made by the original panel was some kind of an arrangement for voluntarily policing this in the music industry as the correct way to go.

If it will help you out in your testimony, I might join Senator Hollings or others in some kind of legislation and/or regulation, unless the free enterprise system, both the producers and you as the performers, see fit to clean up your act.

Mr. ZAPPA. OK, thank you.

The first thing I would like to do, because I know there is some foreign press involved here and they might not understand what the issue is about, one of the things the issue is about is the First Amendment to the Constitution, and it is short and I would like to read it so they will understand. It says:

'Congress shall make no law respecting an establishment of religion or prohibiting the free exercise thereof, or abridging the freedom of speech or of the press or the right of the people peaceably to assemble and to petition the government for a redress of grievances.'

That is for reference.

These are my personal observations and opinions. I speak on behalf of no group or professional organization.

The PMRC proposal is an ill-conceived piece of nonsense which fails to deliver any real benefits to children, infringes the civil liberties of people who are not children, and promises to keep the courts busy for years dealing with the interpretational and enforcemental problems inherent in the proposal's design.

It is my understanding that in law First Amendment issues are decided with a preference for the least restrictive alternative. In this context, the PMRC demands are the equivalent of treating dandruff by decapitation.

No one has forced Mrs. Baker or Mrs. Gore to bring Prince or Sheena Easton into their homes. Thanks to the Constitution, they are free to buy other forms of music for their children.

Apparently, they insist on purchasing the works of contemporary recording artists in order to support a personal illusion of aerobic sophistication. Ladies, please be advised: The $8.98 purchase price does not entitle you to a kiss on the foot from the composer or performer in exchange for a spin on the family Victrola.

Taken as a whole, the complete list of PMRC demands reads like an instruction manual for some sinister kind of toilet training program to house-break all composers and performers because of the lyrics of a few. Ladies, how dare you?

The ladies' shame must be shared by the bosses at the major labels who, through the RIAA, chose to bargain away the rights of composers, performers, and retailers in order to pass H.R. 2911, The Blank Tape Tax, a private tax levied by an industry on consumers for the benefit of a select group within that industry.

Is this a consumer issue? You bet it is. The major record labels need to have H.R. 2911 whiz through a few committees before anybody smells a rat. One of them is chaired by Senator Thurmond. Is it a coincidence that Mrs. Thurmond is affiliated with the PMRC?

I cannot say she is a member, because the PMRC has no members. Their secretary told me on the phone last Friday that the PMRC has no members, only founders. I asked how many other District of Columbia wives are non-members of an organization that raises money by mail, has a tax-exempt status, and seems intent on running the Constitution of the United States through the family paper-shredder. I asked her if it was a cult. Finally, she said she could not give me an answer and that she had to call their lawyer.

While the wife of the Secretary of the Treasury recites "Gonna drive my love inside you" and Senator Gore's wife talks about "bondage" and "oral sex at gunpoint" on the CBS Evening News, people in high places work on a tax bill that is so ridiculous, the only way to sneak it through is to keep the public's mind on something else: Porn rock.

Is the basic issue morality? Is it mental health? Is it an issue at all? The PMRC has created a lot of confusion with improper comparisons between song lyrics, videos, record packaging, radio broadcasting, and live performances. These are all different mediums and the people who work in them have the right to conduct their business without trade-restraining legislation, whipped up like an instant pudding by "The wives of Big Brother."

Is it proper that the husband of a PMRC non-member / founder / person sits on any committee considering business pertaining to the blank tape tax or his wife's lobbying organization? Can any committee thus constituted find facts in a fair and unbiased manner? This committee has three that we know about: Senator Danforth, Senator Packwood, and Senator Gore. For some reason, they seem to feel there is no conflict of interest involved.

Children in the vulnerable age bracket have a natural love for music. If as a parent you believe they should be exposed to something more uplifting than "Sugar Walls," support music appreciation programs in schools. Why have you not considered your child's need for consumer information? Music appreciation costs very little compared to sports expenditures.

Your children have a right to know that something besides pop music exists.

It is unfortunate that the PMRC would rather dispense governmentally sanitized heavy metal music than something more uplifting. Is this an indication of PMRC's personal taste or just another manifestation of the low priority this administration has placed on education for the arts in America?

The answer, of course, is neither. You cannot distract people from thinking about an unfair tax by talking about music appreciation. For that you need sex, and lots of it.

The establishment of a rating system, voluntary or otherwise, opens the door to an endless parade of moral quality control programs based on things certain Christians do not like. What if the next bunch of Washington wives demands a large yellow "J" on all material written or performed by Jews, in order to save helpless children from exposure to concealed Zionist doctrine?

Record ratings are frequently compared to film ratings. Apart from the quantitative difference, there is another that is more important: People who act in films are hired to pretend. No matter how the film is rated, it will not hurt them personally.

Since many musicians write and perform their own material and stand by it as their art, whether you like it or not, an imposed rating will stigmatize them as individuals.
How long before composers and performers are told to wear a festive little PMRC arm band with their scarlet letter on it?

Bad facts make bad law, and people who write bad laws are in my opinion more dangerous than songwriters who celebrate sexuality. Freedom of speech, freedom of religious thought, and the right to due process for composers, performers and retailers are imperiled   if the PMRC and the major labels consummate this nasty bargain.

Are we expected to give up article 1 so the big guys can collect an extra dollar on every blank tape and 10 to 25 percent on tape recorders? What is going on here? Do we get to vote on this tax?

I think that this whole matter has gotten completely blown out of proportion, and I agree with Senator Exon that there is a very dubious reason for having this event. I also agree with Senator Exon that you should not be wasting time on stuff like this, because from the beginning I have sensed that it is somebody's hobby project.

Now, I have done a number of interviews on television. People keep saying, can you not take a few steps in their direction, can you not sympathize, can you not empathize? I do more than that at this point. I have got an idea for a way to stop all this stuff and a way to give parents what they really want, which is information, accurate information as to what is inside the album, without providing a stigma for the musicians who have played on the album or the people who sing it or the people who wrote it. And I think that if you listen carefully to this idea that it might just get by all of the constitutional problems and everything else.

As far as I am concerned, I have no objection to having all of the lyrics placed on the album routinely, all the time. But there is a little problem. Record companies do not own the right automatically to take these lyrics, because they are owned by a publishing company. So, just as all the rest of the PMRC proposals would cost money, this would cost money too, because the record companies would need — they should not be forced to bear the cost, the extra expenditure to the publisher, to print those lyrics.

If you consider that the public needs to be warned about the contents of the records, what better way than to let them see exactly what the songs say? That way you do not have to put any kind of subjective rating on the record. You do not have to call it R, X, D/A, anything. You can read it for yourself.

But in order for it to work properly, the lyrics should be on a uniform kind of a sheet. Maybe even the Government could print those sheets. Maybe it should even be paid for by the Government, if the Government is interested in making sure that people have consumer information in this regard.

And you also have to realize that if a person buys the record and takes it out of the store, once it is out of the store you can't return it if you read the lyrics at home and decide that little Johnny is not supposed to have it.

I think that that should at least be considered, and the idea of imposing these ratings on live concerts, on the albums, asking record companies to re-evaluate or drop or violate contracts that they already have with artists should be thrown out. That is all I have to say.

The CHAIRMAN. Thank you very much, Mr. Zappa. You understand that the previous witnesses were not asking for legislation. And I do not know, I cannot speak for Senator Hollings, but I think the prevailing view here is that nobody is asking for legislation. The question is just focusing on what a lot of people perceive to be a problem, and you have indicated that you at least understand that there is another point of view. But there are people that think that parents should have some knowledge of what goes into their home.

Mr. ZAPPA. All along my objection has been with the tactics used by these people in order to achieve the goal. I just think the tactics have been really bad, and the whole premise of their proposal — they were badly advised in terms of record business law, they were badly advised in terms of practicality, or they would have known that certain things do not work mechanically with what they suggest.

The CHAIRMAN. Senator Gore.

Senator GORE. Thank you very much, Mr. Chairman.

I found your statement very interesting and, although I disagree with some of the statements that you make and have made on other occasions, I have been a fan of your music, believe it or not. I respect you as a true original and a tremendously talented musician.

Your suggestion of printing the lyrics on the album is a very interesting one. The PMRC at one point said they would propose either a rating or warning, or printing all the lyrics on the album. The record companies came back and said they did not want to do that.

I think a lot of people agree with your suggestion that one easy way to solve this problem for parents would be to put the actual words there, so that parents could see them. In fact, the National Association of Broadcasters made exactly the same request of the record companies. I think your suggestion is an intriguing one and might really be a solution for the problem.

Mr. ZAPPA. You have to understand that it does cost money, because you cannot expect publishers to automatically give up that right, which is a right for them. Somebody is going to have to reimburse the publishers, the record industry.

Without trying to mess up the album jacket art, it should be a sheet of paper that is slipped inside the shrink-wrap, so that when you take it out you can still have a complete album package. So there is going to be some extra cost for printing it.

But as long as people realize that for this kind of consumer safety you are going to spend some money and as long as you can find a way to pay for it, I think that would be the best way to let people know.

Senator GORE. I do not disagree with that at all. And the separate sheet would also solve the problem with cassettes as well, because you do not have the space for words on the cassette packs.

Mr. ZAPPA. There would have to be a little accordion-fold.

Senator GORE. I have listened to you a number of times on this issue, and I guess the statement that I want to get from you is whether or not you feel this concern is legitimate. You feel very strongly about your position, and I understand that. You are very articulate and forceful.

But occasionally you give the impression that you think parents are just silly to be concerned at all.

Mr. ZAPPA. No; that is not an accurate impression.

Senator GORE. Well, please clarify it, then.

Mr. ZAPPA. First of all, I think it is the parents' concern; it is not the Government's concern.

Senator GORE. The PMRC agrees with you on that.

Mr. ZAPPA. Well, that does not come across in the way they have been speaking. The whole drift that I have gotten, based upon the media blitz that has attended the PMRC and its rise to infamy, is that they have a special plan, and it has smelled like legislation up until now. There are too many things that look like hidden agendas involved with this. And I am a parent. I have got four children. Two of them are here. I want them to grow up in a country where they can think what they want to think, be what they want to be, and not what somebody's wife or somebody in Government makes them be.

I do not want to have that and I do not think you do either.

Senator GORE. OK. But now you are back on the issue of Government involvement. Let me say briefly on this point that the PMRC says repeatedly no legislation, no regulation, no Government action. It certainly sounded clear to me.

And as far as a hidden agenda, I do not see one, hear one, or know of one.

Mr. ZAPPA. OK, let me tell you why I have drawn these conclusions. First of all, they may say, we are not interested in legislation. But there are others who do, and because of their project bad things have happened in this country in the industry.
I believe there is actually some liability. Look at this. You have a situation where, even if you go for the lyric printed thing in the record, because of the tendency among Americans to be copycats — one guy commits a murder, you get a copycat murder — now you've got copycat censors.

You get a very bad situation in San Antonio, TX, right now where they are trying to pass PMRC-type individual ratings and attach them to live concerts, with the mayor down there trying to make a national reputation by putting San Antonio on the map as the first city in the United States to have these regulations, against the suggestion of the city attorney, who says, I do not think this is constitutional.

But you know, there is this fervor to get in and do even more and even more.
And the other thing, the PMRC starts off talking about lyrics, but when they take it over into other realms they start talking about the videos. In fact, you misspoke yourself at the beginning in your introduction when you were talking about the music does this, the music does that. There is a distinct difference between those notes and chords and the baseline and the rhythm that support the words and the lyrics.

I do not know whether you really are talking about controlling the type of music.

The CHAIRMAN. The lyrics.

Mr. ZAPPA. So specifically we are talking about lyrics. It began with lyrics. But even looking at the PMRC fundraising letter, in the last paragraph at the bottom of the page it starts looking like it is branching into other areas, when it says: "We realize that this material has pervaded other aspects of society." And it is like what, you are going to fix it all for me?

Senator GORE. No. I think the PMRC's acknowledging some of the statements by some of their critics who say: well, why single out the music industry.

Do I understand that you do believe that there is a legitimate concern here?

Mr. ZAPPA. But the legitimate concern is a matter of taste for the individual parent and how much sexual information that parent wants to give their child, at what age, at what time, in what quantity,

OK. And I think that, because there is a tendency in the United States to hide sex, which I think is an unhealthy thing to do, and many parents do not give their children good sexual education, in spite of the fact that little books for kids are available, and other parents demand that sexual education be taken out of school, it makes the child vulnerable, because if you do not have something rational to compare it to when you see or hear about something that is aberrated you do not perceive it as an aberration.

Senator GORE. OK, I have run out of time.

Thank you, Mr. Chairman.

The CHAIRMAN. Senator Rockefeller.

Senator ROCKEFELLER. No questions, Mr. Chairman.

The CHAIRMAN. Senator Gorton.

Senator GORTON. Mr. Zappa, I am astounded at the courtesy and soft-voiced nature of the comments of my friend, the Senator from Tennessee. I can only say that I found your statement to be boorish, incredibly and insensitively insulting to the people that were here previously; that you could manage to give the first amendment of the Constitution of the United States a bad name, if I felt that you had the slightest understanding of it, which I do not.

You do not have the slightest understanding of the difference between Government action and private action, and you have certainly destroyed any case you might otherwise have had with this Senator.

Thank you, Mr. Chairman.

Mr. ZAPPA. Is this private action?

The CHAIRMAN. Senator Exon.

Senator EXON. Mr. Chairman, thank you very much.

Mr. Zappa, let me say that I was surprised that Senator Gore knew and liked your music. I must confess that I have Mr. ZAPPA. I would be more than happy to recite my lyrics to you.

Senator EXON. Can we forgo that? never heard any of your music, to my knowledge.

Senator GORE. You have probably never heard of the *Mothers of Invention.*

Senator EXON. I have heard of Glen Miller and Mitch Miller. Did you ever perform with them?

Mr. ZAPPA. As a matter of fact, I took music lessons in grade school from Mitch Miller's brother.

Senator EXON. That is the first sign of hope we have had in this hearing.

Let us try and get down to a fundamental question here that I would like to ask you, Mr. Zappa. Do you believe that parents have the right and the obligation to mold the psychological development of their children?

Mr. ZAPPA. Yes, I think they have that right, and I also think they have that obligation.
Senator EXON. Do you see any extreme difficulty in carrying out those obligations for a parent by material falling into the hands of their children over which they have little or no control?

Mr. ZAPPA. Well, one of the things that has been brought up before is talking about very young children getting access to the material that they have been showing here today. And what I have said to that in the past is a teenager may go into a record store unescorted with $8.98 in his pocket, but very young children do not.

If they go into a record store, the $8.98 is in mom or dad's pocket, and they can always say, Johnny, buy a book. They can say, Johnny, buy instrumental music; there is some nice classical music for you here; why do you not listen to that.

The parent can ask or guide the child in another direction, away from Sheena Easton, Prince, or whoever else you have been complaining about. There is always that possibility.
Senator EXON. As I understand it from your testimony — and once again, I want to emphasize that I see nothing wrong whatsoever; in fact, I salute the ladies for bringing this to the attention of the public as best they see fit. I think you could tell from my testimony that I tend to agree with them.

I want to be very careful that we do not overstep our bounds and try and – and I emphasize once again – tell somebody else what they should see. I am primarily worried about children. It seems to me from your statement that you have no obligation – or no objection whatsoever to printing lyrics, if that would be legally possible, or from a standpoint of having the room to do that, on records or tapes. Is that not what you said?

Mr. ZAPPA. I think it would be advisable for two reasons. One, it gives people one of the things that they have been asking for. It gives them that type of consumer protection because, if you can read the English language and you can see the lyrics on the back, you have no excuse for complaining if you take the record out of the store.

And also, I think that the record industry has been damaged and it has been given a very bad rap by this whole situation because it has been indicated, or people have attempted to indicate, that there is so much of this kind of material that people object to in the industry, that that is what the industry is.

It is not bad at all. Some of the albums that have been selected for abuse here are obscure. Some of them are already several years old. And I think that a lot of deep digging was done in order to come up with the song about anal vapors or whatever it was that they were talking about before.

Senator EXON. If I understand you, you would be in support of printing the lyrics, but you are adamantly opposed to any kind of a rating system?

Mr. ZAPPA. I am opposed to the rating system because, as I said, if you put a rating on the record it goes directly to the character of the person who made the record, whereas if you rate a film, a guy who is in the film has been hired as an actor. He is pretending. You rate the film, whatever it is, it does not hurt him.

But whether you like what is on the record or not, the guy who made it, that is his art and to stigmatize him is unfair.

Senator EXON. Well, likewise, if you are primarily concerned about the artists, is it not true that for many, many years, we have had ratings of movies with indications as to the sexual content of movies and that has been, as near as I can tell, a voluntary action on the part of the actors in the movies and the producers of the movies and the distributors?

That seems to have worked reasonably well. What is wrong with that?

Mr. ZAPPA. Well, first of all, it replaced something that was far more restrictive, which was the Hayes Office. And as far as that being voluntary, there are people who wish they did not have to rate their films. They still object to rating their films, but the reason the ratings go on is because if they are not rated they will not get distributed or shown in theaters . So there is a little bit of pressure involved, but still there is no stigma.

Senator EXON. The Government does not require that. The point I am trying to make is – and while I think these hearings should not have been held if we are not considering legislation or regulations at this time, I emphasized earlier that they might follow.

I simply want to say to you that I suspect that, unless the industry "cleans up their act" – and I use that in quotes again – there is likely to be legislation. And it seems to me that it would not be too far removed from reality or too offensive to anyone if you could follow the general guidelines, right, wrong, or indifferent, that are now in place with regard to the movie industry.

Mr. ZAPPA. Well, I would object to that. I think first of all, I believe it was you who asked the question of Mrs. Gore whether there was any other indication on the album as to the contents. And I would say that a buzzsaw blade between a guy's legs on the album cover is a good indication that it is not for little Johnny.

Senator EXON. I do not believe I asked her that question, but the point you made is a good one, because if that should not go to little minds I think there should be at least some minimal activity or attempt on the part of the producers and distributors, and indeed possibly the performers, to see that that does not get to that little mind.

Mr. Chairman, thank you very much.

The CHAIRMAN. Senator Hollings.

Senator HOLLINGS. Mr. Zappa, I apologize for coming back in late, but I am just hearing the latter part of it. I hear that you say that perhaps we could print the words, and I think that is a good suggestion, but it is unfair to have albums rated.

Now, it is not considered unfair in the movie industry, and I want you to elaborate. I do not want to belabor you, but why is it unfair? I mean, it is accurate, is it not?

Mr. ZAPPA. Well, I do not know whether it is accurate, because sometimes they have trouble deciding how a film gets to be an X or an R or whatever. And you have two problems. One is the quantity of material, 325 films per year versus 25,000 4-minute songs per year, OK.

You also have a problem that an album is a compilation of different types of cuts. If one song on the album is sexually explicit and all the rest of it sounds like Pat Boone, what do you get on the album? How are you going to rate it?

There are little technical difficulties here, and also you have the problem of having somebody in the position of deciding what's good, what's bad, what's talking about the devil, what is too violent, and the rest of that stuff.

But the point I made before is that when you rate the album you are rating the individual, because he takes personal responsibility for the music; and in the movies, the actors who are performing in the movie, it does not hurt them.

Senator HOLLINGS. Well, very good. I think the actual printing of the content itself is perhaps even better than the rating. Let everyone else decide.

Mr. ZAPPA. I think you should leave it up to the parents, because not all parents want to keep their children totally ignorant.

Senator HOLLINGS. Well, you and I would differ on what is ignorance and education, I can see that. But if it was there, they could see what they were buying and I think that is a step in the right direction.

As Senator Exon has pointed out, the primary movers in this particular regard are not looking for legislation or regulations, which is our function. To be perfectly candid with you, I would look for regulations or some kind of legislation, if it could be constitutionally accomplished, unless of course we have these initiatives from the industry itself.

I think your suggestion is a good one. If you print those words, that would go a long way toward satisfying everyone's objections.

Mr. ZAPPA. All we have to do is find out how it is going to be paid for.

Senator HOLLINGS. Thank you, Mr. Chairman.

The CHAIRMAN. Senator Hawkins.

Senator HAWKINS. Mr. Zappa, you say you have four children?

Mr. ZAPPA. Yes, four children.

Senator HAWKINS. Have you ever purchased toys for those children?

Mr. ZAPPA. No; my wife does.

Senator HAWKINS. Well, I might tell you that if you were to go in a toy store – which is very educational for fathers, by the way; it is not a maternal responsibility to buy toys for children – that you may look on the box and the box says, this is suitable for 5 to 7 years of age, or 8 to 15, or 15 and above, to give you some guidance for a toy for a child.

Do you object to that?

Mr. ZAPPA. In a way I do, because that means that somebody in an office someplace is making a decision about how smart my child is.

Senator HAWKINS. I would be interested to see what toys your kids ever had.

Mr. ZAPPA. Why would you be interested?

Senator HAWKINS. Just as a point of interest.

Mr. ZAPPA. Well, come on over to the house. I will show them to you.

Senator HAWKINS. I might do that.

Do you make a profit from sales of rock records?

Mr. ZAPPA. Yes.

Senator HAWKINS. So you do make a profit from the sales of rock records?

Mr. ZAPPA. Yes.

Senator HAWKINS. Thank you. I think that statement tells the story to this committee. Thank you.

The CHAIRMAN. Mr. Zappa, thank you very much for your testimony.

Mr. ZAPPA. Thank you.

[The statement follows]

STATEMENT OF FRANK ZAPPA

These are my personal observations and opinions. They are addressed to the PMRC as well as this committee. I speak on behalf of no group or professional organization.

The PMRC proposal is an ill-conceived piece of nonsense which fails to deliver any real benefits to children, infringes the civil liberties of people who are not children, and promises to keep the courts busy for years, dealing with the interpretational and enforcemental problems inherent in the proposal's design.

It is my understanding that, in law, First Amendment Issues are decided with a preference for the least restrictive alternative. In this context, the PMRC's demands are the equivalent of treating dandruff by decapitation.

No one has forced Mrs. Baker or Mrs. Gore to bring Prince or Sheena Easton into their homes. Thanks to the Constitution, they are free to buy other forms of music for their children. Apparently, they insist on purchasing the works of contemporary recording artists in order to support a personal illusion of aerobic sophistication. Ladies, please be advised: The $8.98 purchase price does not entitle you to a kiss on the foot from the composer or performer in exchange for a spin on the family Victrola. Taken as a whole, the complete list of PMRC demands reads like an instruction manual for some sinister kind of "toilet training program" to house-break all composers and performers because of the lyrics of a few. Ladies, how dare you?

The ladies' shame must be shared by the bosses at the major labels who, through the RIAA, chose to bargain away the rights of composers, performers, and retailers in order to pass H.R. 2911, The Blank Tape Tax: A private tax levied by an industry on consumers for the benefit of a select group within that industry. Is this a "consumer issue"? You bet it is. PMRC spokesperson, Kandy Stroud, announced to millions of fascinated viewers on last Friday's ABC Nightline debate that Senator Gore, a man she described as "A friend of the music industry," is co-sponsor of something she referred to as "anti-piracy legislation". Is this the same tax bill with a nicer name?

The major record labels need to have H.R. 2911 whiz through a few committees before anybody smells a rat. One of them is chaired by Senator Thurmond. Is it a coincidence that Mrs. Thurmond is affiliated with the PMRC? I cannot say she's a member, because the PMRC has no members. Their secretary told me on the phone last Friday that the PMRC has no members . . . only founders. I asked how many other D.C. wives are non-members of an organization that raises money by mail, has a tax-exempt status, and seems intent on running the Constitution of the United States through the family paper-shredder. I asked her if it was a cult. Finally, she said she couldn't give me an answer and that she had to call their lawyer. While the wife of the Secretary of the Treasury recites "Gonna drive my love inside you . . .", and Senator Gore's wife talks about "Bondage!" and "oral sex at gunpoint," on the CBS Evening News, people in high places work on a tax bill that is so ridiculous, the only way to sneak it through is to keep the public's mind on something else: 'Porn rock'.

The PMRC practices a curious double standard with these fervent recitations. Thanks to them, helpless young children all over America get to hear about oral sex at gunpoint on network TV several nights a week. Is there a secret FCC dispensation here? What sort of end justifies THESE means? PTA parents should keep an eye on these ladies if that's their idea of 'good taste'.

Is the basic issue morality? Is it mental health? Is it an issue at all? The PMRC has created a lot of confusion with improper comparisons between song lyrics, videos, record packaging, radio broadcasting, and live performances. These are all different mediums, and the people who work in them have the right to conduct their business without trade-restraining legislation, whipped up like an instant pudding by The Wives of Big Brother.

Is it proper that the husband of a PMRC non-member/founder/person sits on any committee considering business pertaining to the Blank Tape Tax or his wife's lobbying organization? Can any committee thus constituted 'find facts' in a fair and unbiased manner? This committee has three. A minor conflict of interest?

The PMRC promotes their program as a harmless type of consumer information service providing 'guidelines' which will assist baffled parents in the determination of the 'suitability' of records listened to by 'very young children'. The methods they propose have several unfortunately   side effects, not the least of which is the reduction of all American Music, recorded and live, to the intellectual level of a Saturday morning cartoon show.

Teenagers with $8.98 in their pocket might go into a record store alone, but 'very young children' do not. Usually there is a parent in attendance. The $8.98 is in the parents' pocket. The parent can always suggest that the $8.98 be spent on a book.

If the parent is afraid to let the child read a book, perhaps the $8.98 can be spent on recordings of instrumental music. Why not bring jazz or classical music into your home instead of Blackie Lawless or Madonna? Great music with no words at all is available to anyone with sense enough to look beyond this week's platinum-selling fashion plate.

Children in the 'vulnerable' age bracket have a natural love for music. If, as a parent, you believe they should be exposed to something more uplifting than sugar walls, support Music Appreciation programs in schools. Why haven't you considered your child's need for consumer information? Music Appreciation costs very little compared to sports expenditures. Your children have a right to know that something besides pop music exists.

It is unfortunate that the PMRC would rather dispense governmentally sanitized Heavy Metal Music, than something more 'uplifting'. Is this an indication of PMRC's personal taste, or just another manifestation of the low priority this administration has placed on education for The Arts in America? The answer, of course, is neither. You cannot distract people from thinking about an unfair tax by talking about Music Appreciation. For that you need sex . . . and lots of it.

Because of the subjective nature of the PMRC ratings, it is impossible to guarantee that some sort of 'despised concept' won't sneak through, tucked away in new slang or the overstressed pronunciation of an otherwise innocent word. If the goal here is total verbal/moral safety, there is only one way to achieve it; watch no TV, read no books, see no movies, listen to only instrumental music, or buy no music at all.

The establishment of a rating system, voluntary or otherwise, opens the door to an endless parade of Moral Quality Control Programs based on "Things Certain Christians Don't Like". What if the next bunch of Washington Wives demands a large yellow "J" on all material written or performed by Jews, in order to save helpless children from exposure to 'concealed Zionist doctrine'?

Record ratings are frequently compared to film ratings. Apart from the quantitative difference, there is another that is more important: People who act in films are hired to 'pretend'. No matter how the film is rated, it won't hurt them personally. Since many musicians write and perform their own material and stand by it as their art (whether you like it or not), an imposed rating will stigmatize them as individuals. How long before composers and performers are told to wear a festive little PMRC arm band with their Scarlet Letter on it?

The PMRC rating system restrains trade in one specific musical field: Rock. No ratings have been requested for Comedy records or Country Music. Is there anyone in the PMRC who can differentiate infallibly between Rock and Country Music? Artists in both fields cross stylistic lines. Some artists include comedy material. If an album is part Rock, part Country, part

Comedy, what sort of label would it get? Shouldn't the ladies be warning everyone that inside those Country albums with the American Flags, the big trucks, and the atomic pompadours there lurks a fascinating variety of songs about sex, violence, alcohol, and the devil, recorded in a way that lets you hear every word, sung for you by people who have been to prison and are proud of it.

If enacted, the PMRC program would have the effect of protectionist legislation for the Country Music Industry, providing more security for cowboys than it does for children. One major retail outlet has already informed the Capitol Records sales staff that it would not purchase or display an album with any kind of sticker on it.

Another chain with outlets in shopping malls has been told by the landlord that if it racked "hard-rated albums" they would lose their lease. That opens up an awful lot of shelf space for somebody. Could it be that a certain Senatorial husband and wife team from Tennessee sees this as an 'affirmative action program' to benefit the suffering multitudes in Nashville? Is the PMRC attempting to save future generations from SEX ITSELF? The type, the amount, and the timing of sexual information given to a child should be determined by the parents, not by people who are involved in a tax scheme cover-up.

The PMRC has concocted a Mythical Beast, and compounds the chicanery by demanding 'consumer guidelines' to keep it from inviting your children inside its sugar walls. Is the next step the adoption of a "PMRC National Legal Age For Comprehension of Vaginal Arousal". Many people in this room would gladly support such legislation, but, before they start drafting their bill, I urge them to consider these facts:

1. There is no conclusive scientific evidence to support the claim that exposure to any form of music will cause the listener to commit a crime or damn his soul to hell.
2. Masturbation is not illegal. If it is not illegal to do it, why should it be illegal to sing about it?
3. No medical evidence of hairy palms, warts, or blindness has been linked to masturbation or vaginal arousal, nor has it been proven that hearing references to either topic automatically turns the listener into a social liability.
4. Enforcement of anti-masturbatory legislation could prove costly and time consuming.
5. There is not enough prison space to hold all the children who do it.

The PMRC's proposal is most offensive in its "moral tone". It seems to enforce a set of implied religious values on its victims. Iran has a religious government. Good for them. I like having the capitol of the United States in Washington, DC, in spite of recent efforts to move it to Lynchburg, VA.

Fundamentalism is not a state religion. The PMRC's request for labels regarding sexually explicit lyrics, violence, drugs, alcohol, and especially occult content reads like a catalog of phenomena abhorrent to practitioners of that faith. How a person worships is a private matter, and should not be inflicted upon or exploited by others. Understanding the Fundamentalist leanings of this organization, I think it is fair to wonder if their rating system will eventually be extended to inform parents as to whether a musical group has homosexuals in it. Will the PMRC permit musical groups to exist, but only if gay members don't sing, and are not depicted on the album cover?

The PMRC has demanded that record companies "re-evaluate" the contracts of those groups who do things on stage that THEY find offensive. I remind the PMRC that groups are comprised of individuals. If one guy wiggles too much, does the whole band get an "X"? If the group gets dropped from the label as a result of this 're-evaluation' process, do the other guys in the group who weren't wiggling get to sue the guy who wiggled because he ruined their careers? Do the founders of the tax-exempt organization with no members plan to indemnify record companies for any losses incurred from unfavorably   decided breach of contract suits, or is there a PMRC secret agent in the Justice Department?

Should individual musicians be rated? If so, who is qualified to determine if the guitar player is an "X", the vocalist is a "D/A" or the drummer is a "V". If the bass player (or his Senator) belongs to a religious group that dances around with poisonous snakes, does he get an "O"? What if he has an earring in one ear, wears an Italian Horn around his neck, sings about his astrological sign, practices yoga, reads the Quaballah, or owns a rosary? Will his "occult content" rating go into an old CoIntelPro computer, emerging later as a "fact", to determine if he qualifies for a home-owner loan? Will they tell you this is necessary to protect the folks next door from the possibility of 'devil-worship' lyrics creeping through the wall?
What hazards await the unfortunate retailer who accidently   sells an "O" rated record to somebody's little Johnny? Nobody in Washington seemed to care when Christian Terrorists bombed abortion clinics in the name of Jesus. Will you care when the "Friends of the wives of big brother" blow up the shopping mall?

The PMRC wants ratings to start as of the date of their enactment. That leaves the current crop of 'objectionable material' untouched. What will be the status of recordings from that Golden Era to censorship? Do they become collector's items . . . or will another "fair and unbiased committee" order them destroyed in a public ceremony?

Bad facts make bad law, and people who write bad laws are, in my opinion, more dangerous than songwriters who celebrate sexuality. Freedom of Speech, Freedom of Religious Tthought , and the Right to Due Process for composers, performers and retailers are imperiled if the PMRC and the major labels consummate this nasty bargain. Are we expected to give up Article One so the big guys can collect an extra dollar on every blank tape and 10 to 25% on tape recorders? What's going on here? Do WE get to vote on this tax? There's an awful lot of smoke pouring out of the legislative machinery used by the PMRC to inflate this issue. Try not to inhale it. Those responsible for the vandalism should pay for the damage by voluntarily rating themselves. If they refuse, perhaps the voters could assist in awarding the Congressional "X", the Congressional "D/A", the Congressional "V", and the Congressional "O". Just like the ladies say: these ratings are necessary to protect our children. I hope it's not too late to put them where they really belong.

The CHAIRMAN. The next witness is John Denver.

John, thank you very much for being with us.

STATEMENT OF JOHN DENVER

Mr. DENVER. Good morning, Mr. Chairman. It is a great pleasure to be with you, and I apologize for running in and out. I seem to be testifying and briefing many people here on Capitol Hill today, and it causes the ingoing and outgoing.

Honorable Chairman, members of the committee, ladies and gentlemen: It is a great honor and a privilege to appear before you this morning and to take advantage of the opportunity given me in our free society to speak my mind, to give voice to my opinions in a public forum in front of not only the leadership of our great country, but the press, the media, and through them all who might be listening around our country and around the world.

I am here to address the issue of a possible rating system in the recording industry, labeling records where excesses of explicit sex and graphic violence have occurred and, furthermore, references to drugs and alcohol or the occult are included in the lyrics.

These hearings have been called to determine whether or not the Government should intervene to enforce this practice. Mr. Chairman, this would approach censorship. May I be very clear that I am strongly opposed to censorship of any kind in our society or anywhere else in the world.

I have had in my experience two encounters with this sort of censorship. My song "Rocky Mountain High" was banned from many radio stations as a drug-related song. This was obviously done by people who had never seen or been to the Rocky Mountains and also had never experienced the elation, celebration of life, or the joy in living that one feels when he observes something as wondrous as the Perseides meteor shower on a moonless, cloudless night, when there are so many stars that you have a shadow from the starlight, and you are out camping with your friends, your best friends, and introducing them to one of nature's most spectacular light shows for the very first time.

Obviously, a clear case of misinterpretation. Mr. Chairman, what assurance have I that any national panel to review my music would make any better judgment?

To my knowledge, my movie "Oh God" was not banned in any theaters . However, some newspapers refused to print our advertisements, and some theaters refused to put the name of the film on the marquee.

I do not believe that we were using the name of our Lord in vain. Quite the opposite, we were making a small effort to spread his message that we are here for each other and not against each other.

Discipline and self-restraint when practiced by an individual, a family, or a company is an effective way to deal with this issue. The same thing when forced on a people by their government or, worse, by a self-appointed watchdog of public morals, is suppression and will not be tolerated in a democratic society.

Mr. Chairman, the suppression of the people of a society begins in my mind with the censorship of the written or spoken word. It was so in Nazi Germany. It is so in many places today where those in power are afraid of the consequences of an informed and educated people.

In a mature, incredibly diverse society such as ours, the access to all perspectives of an issue becomes more and more important. Those things which in our experience are undesirable generally prove to be unfurthering   and sooner or later become boring. That process cannot and should not be stifled.

On the other hand, that which is denied becomes that which is most interesting. That which is hidden – excuse me. That which is denied becomes that which is most desired, and that which is hidden becomes that which is most interesting. Consequently, a great deal of time and energy is spent trying to get at what is being kept from you. Our children, our people, our society and the world cannot afford this waste.

It was my pleasure to meet with radio programmers and broadcasters from all over the country this past week in Dallas. They expressed their concern about this issue and the direction in which it seemed to be going. They also expressed their willingness to practice the discipline and self-restraint that I mentioned earlier, especially when they were given direction by their listeners. I believe this to be true, because they are in the business to please their listening audience.

I would like to acknowledge the PMRC for bringing this issue to the attention of not only our industry, but our Government and our people. It is obvious that we are dealing with a real problem which warrants our concern. I would like to point out, however, that we address ourselves not to the problem, but to the symptoms.

I suggest that explicit lyrics and graphic videos are not so far removed from what is seen on television every day and night, whether it be in the soap operas or on the news, and that we should point our finger at the recording industry while watching the general public at a nationally televised baseball game chant in unison "The Blue Jays suck" is ludicrous.

The problem, Mr. Chairman, in my opinion has to do with our willingness as parents to take responsibility for the upbringing of our children, to pay attention to their interests, to respond to their needs, and to recognize that we as parents and as individuals have a greater influence on our children and on each other than anything else could possibly have.

To quote a wise old man from ancient China: "If there be righteousness – " Not self-righteousness; that is not part of the quote. "If there be righteousness in the heart, there will be beauty in the character. If there be beauty in the character, there will be harmony in the home.

If there be harmony in the home, there will be order in the Nation. And if there be order in the Nation, there will be peace in the world."

I thank you very much, Mr. Chairman, if I may add a couple of personal words. I am a father of two children, both adopted, and I have a lot of friends in the music business, other rock performers who have children also, and all of them, including myself, we have a great concern for our children. That is why I am here today.

In my experience, sir, all over the world one of the most interesting things about the music that young people are listening to is it gives us as adults a very clear insight as to what is going on in their minds. We can know what they are thinking by listening to the music that they surround themselves with.

The people that I have had the opportunity to talk with, the troubled children, the teenagers who are considering suicide, what they expressed to me is a real frustration in their lives, an inability to communicate with their parents, an inability to understand or to envision any kind of a possible future because of the nuclear threat that we live under.

They do not see things getting better economically. They do not see things getting better for the small businessman, for the small farmer. They do not see a future for themselves. It is my opinion that it is out of this that some young people put a gun into their mouths and pull the trigger. We can turn this around, sir. We can address the reality of a problem and not deal with just the symptoms, and create not only a better world for our children but for ourselves and all of humanity.

We can end hunger. We can rid the world of nuclear weapons. We can learn to live together as human beings on a planet that travels through the universe, living the example of peace and harmony among all people.

The CHAIRMAN. John, thank you very much for your excellent statement.

You talked about the importance of, in your words, an informed and educated people, and about the importance of communication between parents and their children. And as I understand it, that is exactly the point that was made by the Parents Music Resource Center group that was here earlier. That is, they are not asking for censorship, they are not asking for Government action.

Nobody has proposed that to my knowledge. There is no legislation that is pending that in any way suggests any censorship. The point is not less information. Nobody is trying to prevent rock stars from singing whatever they want or music companies from publishing whatever they want. The question is one of communication and openness.

Senator Exon said earlier, if we are not legislating why have a hearing? Frequently we have oversight hearings in the Congress, and one of the reasons for it is to just air what is going on, to bring it out in the open, to increase information, not to reduce information.

What the mothers are saying is that they do not have sufficient information. They want to know more, they want to be more informed. They do not want less information. They do not want censorship. They want more information. They want to know.

They do not want what goes on in their homes simply to be a matter between the music artist, the rock star, and their 11- or 12-year-old, 13-year-old child. They want to be in on the act, too, and all they want is more information as to what is going on.

And it would seem to me that that is a reasonable request for them to make, that it is reasonable for all of us to be in on the act, rather than just to have almost a private relationship between our kids and somebody outside the home.

Mr. DENVER. I understand, Senator, and I applaud what is taking place here today. My concern is that it sort of feels like, if we are bringing this issue to the Congress through the Senate, there is a very real possibility that legislation is going to be acted upon. I understand that.

The CHAIRMAN. Zero.

Mr. DENVER. But several gentlemen have said that if it looks like it is possible to make legislation, some of you today have said, if it is possible to make legislation that you would go further with this if there is a constitutional way to do that.

The CHAIRMAN. Just believe me, zero chance of legislation. I do not think anybody has introduced a bill, and I do not really think that is a possibility at all.
The only question is, is there a possibility of, first, bringing the issue before the country.

Mr. DENVER. And you have done that and I applaud that.

The CHAIRMAN. Just talk about it and ventilate our concerns.

And secondly, is there a possibility of increasing the information that is available to parents of kids, who have the real responsibility for raising those children and for establishing whatever values those children are going to have?

Mr. DENVER. I understand.

The CHAIRMAN. Senator Hollings.

Senator HOLLINGS. Welcome. I am glad to see you working, in addition to the hunger field, the hunger of the body, and the hunger of the mind, John. I am delighted to work with you on this.

There are some differences. For one thing, as an old trial lawyer, we know well that Clarence Darrow made a 9-hour summation in the Scopes trial. A trial lawyer today is competing with television and television performers. If he makes more than a 9-minute summation, he has lost the jury, his case, and everything else. The parent is in competition with that 6 hours of rock coming over radio and TV.

Now, it is pleasant to talk about parents and their duties and responsibilities, but they are in one heck of a competition out there. We do know that perhaps with television in many, many instances, parents are trying to do their best – in the Hinckley case and what have you – they tried and tried, but did not realize. You say that the parents have a greater influence. Not necessarily so.

An additional point we have to keep in mind is the proposition of the limited use of protected speech in the broadcast media. You mentioned just coming back from the radio and TV broadcasters' convention last week and their tendering self-rule or regulation. Will that discipline develop? It has not. The only censorship movement now is that of our recent group that has gotten any kind of offer or recognition of the problem itself.

We know, talking about free speech, that the broadcast airwaves belong to the people. We will take a radio station in my own backyard using four-letter words. The FCC fined them. That was not unconstitutional. We do have some authorities, we do have some responsibilities there.

They are not all clean-cut John Denvers. On the contrary, I have not listened to too much. It seems like the majority is otherwise.

I think that the aura or atmosphere developing in this particular hearing is developing to make sure that we do not do nothing, or to transmit, rather, back to the original problem, pornography, suicide, all of this other stuff coming out of these records.

Now, the other gentleman said print the words. I rather like that, since I would not have to read it. He would read it one way, obviously, and I would read it differently, and there is that human error involved.

Do you have any recommendation to the committee other than just do nothing? I mean, you have talked in beautiful terms – you are the best I have seen – on peace – and I am not speaking facetiously – the family and responsibility and the wonderful human nature. I am with you on the stars, we are both supporters of Costeau, and I have authored in this particular committee, the oceanography programs.

Barring all of that, are you saying do nothing?

Mr. DENVER. No, sir, I am not saying do nothing. And that is exactly why I am here and why I applaud this hearing and applaud what these ladies, what the PMRC has presented to us.

Senator HOLLINGS. Well, I think we have got to be sensible about it. But like you say – particularly with at least the radio and TV, I cannot read the words coming there. I can see that difference between Mr. Zappa and myself. A person of free volition can go in and read the language and see the words there. I would not have to read it.

Then, to not have some inhibition, some kind of discipline, as you describe it, within the broadcast media, we flunk the course, because there are 6 hours of that thing steaming and beaming into the home.

Mr. DENVER. Well, you know, Senator – excuse me if I am interrupting.

Senator HOLLINGS. No, sir.

Mr. DENVER. When I was raised, television was just coming out and, golly, it was an attractive medium. And I could sit there in front of that TV set and watch it all day. My parents set some restrictions on how much time I could watch television during the week, especially when I was going to school, and I could choose the programs that I wanted to watch.

And I think this is kind of an influence that we can exercise as parents on our children. Just because it is on 7 hours does not mean our kids are going to sit there and watch it that whole time, and we can give them a certain amount of time.

And over here, for me one of the things that I am fortunate with is my children and I live in a beautiful country and we have a lot of activities which really call us outdoors, call us together and away from the boob tube. I do not watch very much television.

And I think we can exercise this kind of influence on our children in a city environment.

Senator HOLLINGS. You and I are different – I mean, you and I are the same. We do not watch much TV. I do not watch that much television, obviously.

But the record is otherwise. They are watching television as much as the instructions in the classrooms of the public schools and more. All surveys show that, so it is being watched. That is the fact, and living in the real world, where you and I would like to restrict our children and my grandchildren now, it is a real problem. It is a real problem.

And I guess you know from being a master at the art that, where you start off selling that record is to get it accepted at some good programming, some good broadcasting, and then the sales follow. You cannot print those words ahead of time so I will know to cut the television off quick.

Whatever it is, unless that discipline develops, in other words, with the broadcast media, we are going to be forced somewhere with regulations, through the FCC or otherwise. I do not think the American public is going to go along just with a nice hearing up in Washington. I think there is going to have to be something more developed and some kind of discipline, as you indicate.

I am trying to find out from you, how you develop that discipline a little bit better than what has been developed?

Mr. DENVER. Well, I think that a good beginning to addressing this real problem is this hearing that is taking place. What most concerns me, aside from potential legislation which might be enacted, which we have heard today is not going to be the case, is that the whole presentation by the PMRC comes from in my experience a foundation of fear.

The only thing we have to fear, as President Roosevelt said, is fear itself. I am not afraid of anything. I am not afraid of what my children might see. I am not afraid of anything that might be shown them or done in their presence that would lessen my influence on them or their opportunity to grow, to be fine upstanding adults, and perhaps someday serve in this very august body.

Senator HOLLINGS. Well, most respectfully, President Roosevelt never heard these records.

The CHAIRMAN. Senator Gore.

Mr. DENVER. I think the things that he heard were far worse, sir.

The CHAIRMAN. Senator Gore.

Senator GORE. Thank you very much, Mr. Chairman.

It is an honor   to be able to ask some questions. I have been a fan for a long time, Mr. Denver, not only of your music but also of your contributions to efforts such as Farm Aid at the present time, world peace, and your trips to the Soviet Union and elsewhere.

Do you see the trend of increased sexual explicitness and violence in some rock music that is outlined by this presentation? Have you ever been to a *Motley Crue* concert, for example?

Mr. DENVER. No, sir.

Senator GORE. Do you agree that there does seem to be a growing trend, at least in the heavy metal area, that emphasizes explicit violence and sex and sado-masochism and the rest? You are aware of that music, are you not?

Mr. DENVER. Yes.

Senator GORE. Why do you think that has been growing in popularity?

Mr. DENVER. Again, sir, my experience, not only in this country but all over the world, is that music today is that medium which most specifically tells us what is going on in young people's minds, not what is being put into them but what reflects what they are interested in. I think that this addresses itself to a much graver problem in fact, the source of the symptom that we are discussing here today.

Senator GORE. Well, if a 10-year-old listens to a song glorifying rape, that is not reflecting what is in that 10-year-old's mind, is it?

Mr. DENVER. I do not think so. I do not think there are many 10-year-olds who know what rape is.

Senator GORE. I am not sure I would agree with that.

If you have an explicit description of a suicide, in a song that seems to glorify and promote suicide, young people are aware of that.

Mr. DENVER. Senator Gore, excuse me for interrupting. If I could count the number of times that a mother or father has come up to me or a child has come up to me and said, if I do not get your autograph my mother is going to kill me, if I do not get your autograph my daughter is going to kill me – you know, just this is a part of our language. And there might be a slight difference, but I do not think it is as big as you point out.

In a way, this video that we watched here today I think is probably a fantasy that every kid has about his father at some point in time. It may not be exactly those particular graphics. It may be out on the farm and being able to take your dad out and put a board to his fanny. But this goes on. This is a part of growing up.

And our society has gotten increasingly complex. There are many more images to reach from. They all have an impact on the child's mind.

And I am saying that the small percentage of records that we are discussing here today compared to the 125,000 songs that are released every year is miniscule and it is not going to affect our children to a degree that we need to be fearful of.

We need to be conscious of it. We need to concern ourselves and we need to communicate with our children and have them feel comfortable with communicating with us.

Senator GORE. Let me come back to the question about suicide. Let us say you have a popular rock star who has a lot of fans, who sings a song that says suicide is the solution, and appears in fan magazines with a gun barrel pointed in his mouth and promotes material that seems to glorify suicide.

The United States has one of the highest rates of teen suicide of any country in the world. The rate has gone up 300 percent in the last decade among young people, while it has remained constant among adults.

Do you think it is a responsible act for a record company to put out a song glorifying suicide and for the artist to promote the album by putting a gun in his mouth in a simulation of suicide?

Mr. DENVER. I would not like to be the one to tell a record company or an artist what to do. I certainly think the picture you have described is deplorable, and if I found that in my home I would talk to my kids about it and get rid of it.

The CHAIRMAN. Could I interrupt? It is my understanding that you have to leave. Is that correct?

Mr. DENVER. Senator, I appreciate that. Yes, I have an appointment with NASA at noon and if it is possible I would like to go to that. But I also really appreciate being able to discuss this with you all and I am happy to stay.

The CHAIRMAN. Let me ask, are there any more questions?

Senator GORE. Mr. Chairman, I will stop my questions at this time and wish Mr. Denver good luck in getting on the Space Shuttle.

Mr. DENVER. Thanks very much. I appreciate that.

The CHAIRMAN. Senator Exon has a question and I think Senator Pressler has.
Senator EXON. Mr. Denver, thank you very much for being here. I appreciated your testimony. I do not know you, but, although it may lead to the beginning of the end of your career, I like your music.

Senator EXON. In fact, I think I know you. I think a friend of yours, Rainbow Terrain, has talked about you. She is an art instructor and a friend of my wife's, and I kind of think I know you through her.

Just one basic question. Please clarify for us, what is your opinion to the key question that has been asked time and time again here, and you have alluded to it: Are you for the printing of material on records? Are you for or against, or are you for or against any kind of a rating as long as it is done voluntarily between the record companies and the producers?
That is my key question. And I would simply say one more time, which I have said every time I have had this microphone this morning, I think it is wrong to imply that, although no bills have been introduced, that bills might not be introduced. And I want to hold that threat, for what it is worth, over the head of trying to accomplish some free enterprise volunteerism that most people have agreed to.

What do you think about a free enterprise volunteerism, getting together and either printing or coming up with a rating program of some kind that would be properly displayed in the records?

Mr. DENVER. I am opposed. As an artist, I am opposed to any kind of a rating system, voluntarily or otherwise. I think putting lyrics on the sleeve of an album or a jacket of an album is no problem for me.

Again, I think it goes beyond reading the words, and I bring up again the song "Rocky Mountain High." You know, some people, high is high, and high is getting stoned and high is a feeling of elation, celebration of life.

As I told the people of the Soviet Union when I had the privilege of singing for them there, I sang "Rocky Mountain High" and then I described what "high" meant to me. And I said to them, that is how I feel having the privilege of singing for you.

That is how I feel having the opportunity to participate in my Government here today.

Senator EXON. Thank you, Mr. Denver.

The CHAIRMAN. Senator Pressler.

Senator PRESSLER. I guess that ties in with my question. Your basic line is that you are against any type of Government action in this area, or indeed any voluntary labeling?

Mr. DENVER. I would be, yes.

Senator PRESSLER. Thank you very much.

The CHAIRMAN. John, thank you very much. Thank you for your patience, for waiting so long.

Mr. DENVER. Thank you, Senator. It is a great privilege to be with you all.

The CHAIRMAN. Thank you.

Next we have Mr. Dee Snider of Twisted Sister, Freefall Talent Group.

Mr. Snider, thank you for being here.

STATEMENT OF DEE SNIDER, OF *TWISTED SISTER*

MR. SNIDER. Thank you for having me here.

I do not know if it is morning or afternoon. I will say both. Good morning and good afternoon.

My name is Dee Snider. That is S-n-i-d-e-r. I have been asked to come here to present my views on "the subject of the content of certain sound recordings and suggestions that recording packages be labeled   to provide a warning to prospective purchasers of sexually explicit or other potentially offensive content."

Before I get into that, I would like to tell the committee a little bit about myself. I am 30 years old, I am married, I have a 3-year-old son. I was born and raised a Christian and I still adhere to those principles. Believe it or not, I do not smoke, I do not drink, and I do not do drugs. I do play in and write the songs for a rock and roll band named *Twisted Sister* that is classified as heavy metal, and I pride myself on writing songs that are consistent with my above-mentioned beliefs.

There are many facets to this complex issue and time does not permit me to address all of them. However, my feelings are expressed for the most part by the August 5, 1985, letter1 to the Parents Music Resource Center   from Mr. Stanley Gortikov, president of the Recording Industry Association of America.

This letter was a formal response to the PMRC petition of the RIAA. The only part of this document I do not support is Mr. Gortikov's unnecessary and unfortunate decision to agree to a so-called generic label on some selected records. In my opinion this should be retracted. Since I seem to be the only person addressing this committee today who has been a direct target of accusations from the presumably responsible PMRC, I would like to use this occasion to speak on a more personal note and show just how unfair the whole concept of lyrical interpretation and judgment can be and how many times this can amount to little more than character assassination.

I have taken the liberty of distributing to you material and lyrics pertaining to these accusations. There were three attacks in particular which I would like to address.

- **Accusation No. 1.**

This attack was contained in an article written by Tipper Gore, which was given the forum of a full page in my hometown newspaper on Long Island. In this article Ms. Gore claimed that one of my songs, "Under the Blade," had lyrics encouraging sadomasochism, bondage, and rape.

The lyrics she quoted have absolutely nothing to do with these topics. On the contrary, the words in question are about surgery and the fear that it instills   in people. Furthermore, the reader of this article is led to believe that the three lines she quotes go together in the song when, as you can see, from reading the lyrics, the first two lines she cites are an edited phrase from the second verse and the third line is a misquote of a line from the chorus.

That the writer could misquote me is curious, since we make it a point to print all our lyrics on the inner sleeve of every album. As the creator of "Under the Blade," I can say categorically that the only sadomasochism, bondage, and rape in this song is in the mind of Ms. Gore.]

- **Accusation No. 2.**

The PMRC has made public a list of 15 of what they feel are some of the most blatant songs lyrically. On this list is our song "We're Not Gonna Take It," upon which has been bestowed a "V" rating, indicating violent lyrical content.

You will note from the lyrics before you that there is absolutely no violence of any type either sung about or implied anywhere in the song. Now, it strikes me that the PMRC may have confused our video presentation for this song with the song with the lyrics, with the meaning of the lyrics.

It is no secret that the videos often depict story lines completely unrelated to the lyrics of the song they accompany. The video "We're Not Gonna Take It" was simply meant to be a cartoon with human actors playing variations on the Roadrunner/Wile E. Coyote theme, Each stunt was selected from my extensive personal collection of cartoons.

You will note when you watch the entire video that after each catastrophe our villain suffers through, in the next sequence he reappears unharmed by any previous attack, no worse for the wear.

By the way, I am very pleased to note that the United Way of America has been granted a request to use portions of our "We're Not Gonna Take It" video in a program they are producing on the subject of the changing American family. They asked for it because of its "light-hearted way of talking about communicating with teenagers."

It is gratifying that an organization as respected as the United Way of America appreciates where we are coming from. I have included a copy of the United Way's request as part of my written testimony. Thank you, United Way.

• **Accusation No. 3.**
Last Tuesday a public forum regarding the lyric controversy was held in New York. Among the panelists was Ms. Gore. Trying to stem the virtual tidal wave of anti-ratings sentiment coming from the audience, Ms. Gore made the following statement:

I agree this is a small percentage of all music, thank goodness. But it is becoming more mainstream. You look at even the t-shirts that kids wear and you see *Twisted Sister* and a woman in handcuffs sort of spread-eagled.

This is an outright lie. Not only have we never sold a shirt of this type; we have always taken great pains to steer clear of sexism in our merchandise, records, stage show, and personal lives. Furthermore, we have always promoted the belief that rock and roll should not be sexist, but should cater to males and females equally.

I feel that an accusation of this type is irresponsible, damaging to our reputation, and slanderous. I defy Ms. Gore to produce such a shirt to back up her claim. I am tired of running into kids on the street who tell me that they cannot play our records anymore because of the misinformation their parents are being fed by the PMRC on TV and in the newspapers. These are the only three accusations I have come across. All three are totally unfounded. Who knows what other false and irresponsible things may have been said about me or my band. There happens to be one area where I am in complete agreement with the PMRC, as well as the National PTA and probably most of the parents on this committee. That is, it is my job as a parent to monitor what my children see, hear, and read during their preteen years. The full responsibility for this falls on the shoulders of my wife and I, because there is no one else capable of making these judgments for us.

Parents can thank the PMRC for reminding them that there is no substitute for parental guidance. But that is where the PMRC's job ends.

The beauty of literature, poetry, and music is that they leave room for the audience to put its own imagination, experiences, and dreams into the words. The examples I cited earlier showed clear evidence of *Twisted Sister's* music being completely misinterpreted and unfairly judged by supposedly well-informed adults.

We cannot allow this to continue. There is no authority who has the right or the necessary insight to make these judgments, not myself, not the Federal Government, not some recording industry committee, not the PTA, not the RIAA, and certainly not the PMRC.

I would like to thank the committee for this time, and I hope my testimony will aid you in clearing up this issue.

The CHAIRMAN. Thank you, Mr. Snider.

Mr. Snider, let us suppose that there is music which, say, glorifies incest; not yours, but suppose that there is some music that glorifies incest. Do you think parents should know about it, or do you think that it is just a matter between whoever is selling the record and whoever is buying it?

Mr. SNIDER. As I said in my testimony, I think it is very important that parents be aware that these lyrics exist.

The CHAIRMAN. How could they find out about it?

Mr. SNIDER. Well, quite simply, as a parent myself and as a rock fan, I know that when I see an album cover with a severed goat's head in the middle of a pentagram between a woman's legs, that is not the kind of album I want my son to be listening to.
If I read a title on the back of, say, Somebody's Ice Cream Castle, a title called "If the Kid Can't Make You Come," whatever it is, I realize that is a sexually explicit song. By just looking at the cover, looking at the lyrics, looking at, I should say, the titles, that should cover just about all bases.

The few albums that do not express their intentions on the cover or in the song titles, I think a parent could take it home, listen to it. And I do not think there are too many retail stores that would deny them the ability to return the album for something different.

The CHAIRMAN. Do you think that most parents, or even kids for that matter, know everything that is on an album when they buy it, when the child buys the album?

Mr. SNIDER. I do not know half the things that are on half the albums I own. Some of the bands I listen to, I listen for musical reasons. Other bands I listen to for lyrical reasons.

I know that *AC/DC*, one of my favorite bands, sings a lot of songs glorifying hell and damnation. I am a Christian. I do not believe – I do not want to go to hell and I do not want to be damned for all time. But I do like the feel of the songs. The lyrics have no effect on me. Other bands who have more to say, I listen to their words and I learn from their words.

The CHAIRMAN. Do you think that now there is adequate basis for parents to know what is on the records that their kids are buying?

Mr. SNIDER. I think if they really are concerned, there is. But quite honestly, I do not think that the majority of parents are in reality as concerned as the PMRC or myself. I do not think they really want to spend the time to listen to what they might consider to be a bunch of noise. They put it on and they cannot understand a thing that is being said anyway.
And so I think most of them do not spend enough time with it.

The CHAIRMAN. Senator Hollings.

Senator HOLLINGS. Yes. Mr. Snider, I think I would just take the opportunity to make an observation. You and I would differ as to what is obscene or what is shocking or what is vulgar, and persons of goodwill will differ on that particular score.

I think that somewhere in this hearing record, we should not be on the defensive and we should not create the atmosphere that we are powerless. The absolute nature of your statement that we do not have any authority – I only want to refer everyone to the Pacifica Foundation case, where the Federal Communications Commission was questioned as to its power to regulate public radio and TV broadcasts that was indecent but not obscene.

You see, they differed between what was indecent, what was obscene, and what was shocking. They had the seven dirty words. I think everyone remembers that case on the west coast, and the Supreme Court of the United States found that the FCC positively had the authority, and the responsibility.

I am quoting from the language of the Supreme Court:

Patently offensive, indecent material presented over the airwaves confronts the citizen not only in public, but also in the privacy of the home. The individual's right to be left alone, plainly outweighs the first amendment rights of an intruder.

This is not just a forum to rally one way or the other and hope something happens. This is a forum with a definite responsibility with respect to Congress in enunciating the duties of the Federal Communications Commission, which have been constitutionally followed.

I understand your opinion. That is why we invited you up here, to hear your words and not mine. I think that the general nature of all of this testimony of noting censorship, and first amendment absolutism, does not pertain with respect to the broadcast media. That is, of course, the main media that I guess you would agree to actually sell the records, would it not be?

Mr. SNIDER. Yes. Except I would like to clarify something. I said no authority has the right or necessary insight. I did not say you were not able to. I said you do not have the right or I do not have the right or the RIAA.

Also, we are talking about the airwaves as opposed to a person going with their money to purchase an album to play in their room, in their home, on their own time. The airwaves are something different.

I think that the FCC and even MTV have done a fair job in keeping profanity and obscenity and things like that off the public airwaves. But as far as what you listen to in your own home, that is something totally different, I feel in my opinion.

Senator HOLLINGS. I think that the record ought to be elaborated to show just that. Previously, about 5 or 6 years ago, we had the TV networks before this committee, and pursuant to that particular hearing they then came back. I remember CBS specifically. They demonstrated how they had this film, and then got together with the producer and removed certain scenes of violence and certain four-letter words, and did not offend the producer's sense of art in the production itself.

We have made some progress. The bottom line with respect to these particular records, the Supreme Court has found, is that there is that right and that responsibility.

Thank you, Mr. Chairman.

The CHAIRMAN. Senator Gore.

Senator GORE. Thank you very much, Mr. Chairman.

Mr. SNIDER. Excuse me. Are you going to tell me you are a big fan of my music as well?

Senator GORE. No, I am not a fan of your music. I am aware that Frank Zappa and John Denver cover quite a spectrum, and I do enjoy them both. I am not, however, a fan of *Twisted Sister* and I will readily say that.

Mr. Snider, what is the name of your fan club?

Mr. SNIDER. The fan club is called the SMF Fans of *Twisted Sister*.

Senator GORE. And what does "SMF" stand for when it is spelled out?

Mr. SNIDER. It stands for the Sick Mother Fucking Fans of *Twisted Sister*.

Senator GORE. Is this also a Christian group?

Mr. SNIDER. I do not believe profanity has anything to do with Christianity, thank you.

Senator GORE. It is just an interesting choice. I was getting the impression from your presentation that you were a very wholesome kind of performer, and that is an interesting title for your fan club.

You say your song "Under the Blade" is about surgery. Have you ever had surgery with your hands tied and your legs strapped?

Mr. SNIDER. The song was written about my guitar player, Eddie Ojeda. He was having polyps removed from his throat and he was very fearful of this operation. And I said: Eddie, while you are in the hospital I am going to write a song for you.

I said it was about the fear of operations. I think people imagine being helpless on a table, the bright light in their face, the blade coming down on them, and being totally afraid that they may wake up, who knows, dead, handicapped. There is a certain fear of hospitals. That is what, in my imagination, what I see the hospitals like.

Senator GORE. Is there a reference to the hospital in the song?

Mr. SNIDER. No, there is not. But there is not a reference to a woman, sado-masochism, or -- well, bondage, yes.

Senator GORE. There is just a reference to someone whose hands are tied down and whose legs are strapped down, and he is going under the blade to be cut.

Mr. SNIDER. Yes, there is.

Senator GORE. So it is not really a wild leap of the imagination to jump to the conclusion that the song is about something other than surgery or hospitals, neither of which are mentioned in the song?

Mr. SNIDER. No, it is not a wild jump. And I think what I said at one part was that songs allow a person to put their own imagination, experiences, and dreams into the lyrics. People can interpret it in many ways.

Ms. Gore was looking for sado-masochism and bondage and she found it. Someone looking for surgical references would have found that as well.

Senator GORE. Why do you think there is so much sado-masochism and bondage in some of these new songs?

Mr. SNIDER. I cannot speak for the other artists. I am really only here to defend myself, and hopefully by speaking for myself as one person, songwriter in a band that I feel has been unjustly dumped on, that will just warn us of the dangers of what we are trying to do here. I really cannot speak for the other bands.

Senator GORE. Now, you made reference to a comment about T-shirts. I would simply note for the record that the word "T-shirts" was in plural, and one of them referred to *Twisted Sister* and the other referred to a woman in handcuffs. And it was not intended, as I understand it, to say that you appear with a woman in handcuffs.

There are a lot of different T-shirts and advertisements around today. I have noticed from some of the fan magazines particularly featuring heavy metal music that little sado-masochistic outfits are advertised, with the fingerless gloves and spikes and studs on them, and that these little S&M outfits are marketed to teens and preteens. Is that correct?

Mr. SNIDER. Well, they are marketed. Who buys them I am not sure.

I would just like to say, in reference to the comment about T-shirts, I have with me a taped cassette of the exact –

Senator GORE. No, I am reading from your transcript of it in your statement.

Mr. SNIDER. I will have to check the transcript, but when it was said there was no question she was referring to a Twisted Sister T-shirt. There was no question if I played the tape for anybody.

Senator GORE. Well, in your own transcript it is in plural, "T-shirts," and two examples are cited. But I do not want to belabor   that point.

Now, you said that you can look at the titles of albums and look at the covers and tell what kind of material is inside. Does the title "Purple Rain" give you an indication that the material is about masturbation?

Mr. SNIDER. You mean the album title "Purple Rain"? No, it does not. I did not say in all cases. I believe I covered that there are occasional albums that are a bit misleading. I said I do not think a store would refuse a parent who came in and said, "I do not like what is on this record. I would like my money back."

Senator GORE. So the choice the parent has, then, is to sit down and listen to every song on the album; right?

Mr. SNIDER. Or read the lyrics if they are on the record.

Senator GORE. I think that is pretty general agreement that if the lyrics are printed that is one possible solution for this.

Let us suppose the lyrics are not printed. Then what choice does a parent have? To sit down and listen to every song on the album?

Mr. SNIDER. Well, if they are really concerned about it I think that they have to.

Senator GORE. Do you think it is reasonable to expect parents to do that?

Mr. SNIDER. Being a parent is not a reasonable thing. It is a very hard thing. I am a parent and I know. OK. I am a new parent. I only have one child, maybe. But I am learning that there is a lot to being a parent that you did not expect. It is not just always a cute baby. There is a lot of labor, a lot of time, and a lot of effort that goes into it. It is not totally pleasurable.

Senator GORE. And you will find when they get a little bit older that when they are exposed to the kinds of themes that we were presented with earlier, if you love your child you are going to be concerned about that. And if you want to protect that child from unnecessary exposure to inappropriate material, you sometimes need a little help, the kind of guidance that is presented in the movie industry.

It is totally unreasonable in my view to expect parents to sit down and listen to every single song in the albums that their children buy in order to fulfill their responsibilities as parents. Now, the only thing in your statement that I felt at all comfortable about was when you said you shared some of the concerns of the PMRC. I would simply conclude by expressing the hope that artists and the record companies will find a way to manifest that mutual concern in some self-restraint, and show a responsibility and give parents a break.

You are right: it is tough being a parent. It is even tougher being a kid. And if both are going to be able to deal with the kind of material that is coming out in popular music, it seems to me the industry has a responsibility to give them a little help.

Thank you, Mr. Chairman.

The CHAIRMAN. Senator Rockefeller.

Senator ROCKEFELLER. Mr. Snider, do you feel that you have a responsibility as an artist to those who would hear those words that you write?

Mr. SNIDER. I feel a tremendous responsibility. And as I said, I do not put anything down on a record that I cannot stand behind 100 percent. I do not sing about drugs, sex, alcohol. I do not advocate sexism, the use of drugs and drinking, and so I do not write about those things. I only write about things I believe in.

Senator ROCKEFELLER. And that is the way you define what your responsibility is – that is, not to write about things that you do not believe in?

Mr. SNIDER. Yes; I would say to write about things that you can stand behind. I feel myself to be a moral person and I think that I have a lot of positive things to tell people about. And like I said, everything on my records I will stand behind and say, "Yes, I wrote those words and this is what it meant and this is what I was trying to say – Yes."

Senator ROCKEFELLER. Do you think that parents, not only those who are in PMRC but other parents who are concerned here and across the country about the development of new trends in music and the lyrics that go along with that music, are naive or somehow missing the point?

Do you think that they are unduly worried about some of these writings about sado-masochism, suicide, rape, and other things? Do you think that this is not really a serious problem for this country and our young people?

Mr. SNIDER. That is sort of a multiple question. I do not think they are naive and I do not think that at times they are unduly worried. But I do think sometimes they take it overly serious.

I mean, there are monster movies on all the time, they have been going on for ages, and people watch a monster movie and they get scared, and they walk away and it was just a movie. Rock and roll many times is the same thing, to try to get an effect of either laughter, sadness. A lot of the heavy metal bands are trying to scare people and just make them scared like a horror movie.

Vincent Price is not having problems because he has done all of these monster pictures. He is just an actor. I am not going to say I am just an actor, but I am entertaining people and a lot of these bands are entertaining people.

And when they were reading some of these lyrics before, I could not help but laugh. I mean, I had not heard some of them, but some of the lyrics were ridiculously ridiculous. I mean, a kid, even a kid reading that I think would go, oh my God, what is going on? It is ridiculous is the only word I can think of, some of the lyrics.

Senator ROCKEFELLER. In the vehemence with which you attacked Senator Gore's wife, I detected a defensiveness somehow on your part, a lack of assuredness on where you stand on this. Why did you feel it necessary to attribute some of the qualities to her that you did? Why was that important to your testimony?

Mr. SNIDER. First of all, I was not attacking Senator Gore's wife. I was attacking a member of the PMRC.

Senator ROCKEFELLER. You were attacking Senator Gore's wife by name.

Mr. SNIDER. Her name is Tipper Gore, is it not? I did not say the Senator's wife. I said Tipper Gore.

Second, defensive. I have been working very hard. I believe in the music that I play. I believe we have a very bad reputation and I have been doing a lot on my part to try and say, hey, this is not a bad thing, this is fun, this is fantasy.

Kids are coming out, they are screaming, they are yelling, they are letting out their emotions, and they are going home, they are feeling better because they let out a lot of their frustrations. As I said, I pride myself on writing lyrics that are not offensive and that are saying something positive. Most of our songs are about personal freedom. And when somebody tells me, after all I have done to fight against sexism, that I have a shirt with a spread-eagled woman –

Senator ROCKEFELLER. All you have done to what?

Mr. SNIDER. All I have done to fight sexism. The whole *Twisted Sister* thing is very ambiguous: guys wearing makeup. We do not act like women; we act like men. We do not cater to the males or females in the audience. It is just one audience.

So when someone says there is a song about sado-masochism and bondage, or someone says "We're Not Gonna Take It" is violent lyrical content, which is what it has been rated for, yes, I am defensive. Yes, that gets me angry. I am trying to get adults to see that heavy metal is not totally a bad thing.

Senator ROCKEFELLER. How many months in the course of a year do you spend on the road away from home?

Mr. SNIDER. In the course of a year, it would be tough to say. Over a 2-year period, I would spend about 11 months on the road and 18 months at home recording albums, things like that, doing videos.

Senator ROCKEFELLER. Eleven months on the road in a 2-year period?

Mr. SNIDER. Yes, because you do a tour and then you go and record albums. I have been off the road now for 10 months.

Senator ROCKEFELLER. Do you take your child with you?

Mr. SNIDER. He comes sometimes.

Senator ROCKEFELLER. Nine years from now when your child is 12 and in school, will you take your child with you?

Mr. SNIDER. Absolutely.

Senator ROCKEFELLER. When your child is in school?

Mr. SNIDER. Oh, no. Thank you for clarifying. No, I would not take him out of school.

Senator ROCKEFELLER. Then how would it be possible for you to, as a responsible parent, to spend the time that you suggest listening to these records and finding out what it is that you want your son to listen to and what you do not want him to listen to?

Mr. SNIDER. To be perfectly honest, 9 years from now I am going to be well retired and I will be spending more time with my son than any other parent probably ever spends. And that is one of the beautiful things about rock and roll, is that I can retire hopefully at a very early age.

But even now, I am very lucky that I have a wife who I have been going with for 10 years now, we have been married for 4, who is the most incredible mother. And while I am gone, she fills the role, and has a very difficult job, too, of mother and father.

Senator ROCKEFELLER. Do you expect later on, then, that she will be going through these records?

Mr. SNIDER. I think both of us will be doing that.

Senator ROCKEFELLER. Do you expect me to believe that?

Mr. SNIDER. You can. I am terminally teenage. I will be listening to my son's records.

Senator ROCKEFELLER. What about families where both parents have to work, which is an increasing phenomenon in this country now, because they have to survive? And the whole notion of parents sitting down and listening to record after record, tape after tape – that is what you suggested – does that not strike you as just a little bit naive and unrealistic?

Mr. SNIDER. No, it does not, because I know the reality of the record-buying market as a record buyer. With my allowance, I was able to, if I was lucky, afford maybe one album a week at the most. Usually it was one a month. Albums cost anywhere from $6 to $10, and that is a lot of money to a teenager, or to a pre-teenager it is a ridiculous sum.

And to a teenage kid that is a considerable amount of money. And so to listen to one record a week, I do not consider that a hardship.

Senator ROCKEFELLER. Might I ask just one final question, Mr. Chairman?

The CHAIRMAN. Bearing in mind that it is 12:30 and we have a lot of witnesses left, yes.

Senator ROCKEFELLER. I will bear that in mind and will not ask the question.

The CHAIRMAN. Senator Pressler.

Senator PRESSLER. Basically, I want to get down to your recommendations in terms of governmental action, either by this committee or by any Government body. You would recommend no governmental action in this area?

Mr. SNIDER. Absolutely.

Senator PRESSLER. What about industry actions? Would you recommend any type of voluntary labeling ?

Mr. SNIDER. I do not feel that the industry – it has been expressed by many other people that each artist has an individual agreement. One of the big things is artistic freedom in your contract. I do not think the industry can pass a ruling on that.

Senator PRESSLER. And so your legislative recommendations, would that apply just to -- not to broadcast? You would put broadcast and things that are over the airwaves in a different category than things people buy and show in their homes?

Mr. SNIDER. Well, I think we are talking about the purchase of albums and the lyrical content on the albums. That is what I am directing it to at this time.

Senator PRESSLER. So you would disagree with any action on those albums, be they by private industry or Government, any type of labeling ?

Mr. SNIDER. If somebody would ask me what my opinion was, I had said earlier that I did not think there would be a problem for a parent to return an album they had taken home and found it dissatisfactory. I would like to believe that, but some retail stores will give you a hassle if you try to return an open album.

If you want a solution, maybe they could bring back – in the fifties, you could listen to an album in the store before you purchased the album. Most record stores play the albums in the store, and there is usually a stack of those albums opened already that, if you want to go over and take a glance at the cover, which I have done many times myself, you could go over and do that.

So if you want to take some sort of industry action, I would think it would be to force the retail stores to allow people to return product that they are not satisfied with: satisfaction guaranteed.

Senator PRESSLER. Thank you very much.

The CHAIRMAN. Mr. Snider, thank you very much.

Mr. SNIDER. Thank you for your time.

[The material referred to follows]

Mary Elizabeth "Tipper" Gore (née Aitcheson; born August 19, 1948) is an author, photographer, former second lady of the United States, and the wife of Al Gore, from whom she is currently separated. She became well known for her role in the Parents Music Resource Center (PMRC), criticizing music with profane language and promoting Parental Advisory stickers (nicknamed "Tipper Stickers") on record covers, especially in the heavy metal, punk and hip hop genres.

Viewpoints

The Smut and Sadism of Rock
Porno rock is not only sexually explicit; songs and videos celebrate torture, incest and even suicide and murder. The music business should clean up its act.
By Tipper Gore

Sexual innuendo or rebellion has always been a part of rock 'n' roll, but nowadays, sex is described explicitly, complete with moans and groans. Moreover, sadomasochism, bondage, incest and rape are out of the closet and into the lyrics. Whips, chains, handcuffs and leather masks are being popularized in songs and as images in videos and on album covers. Lyrics glorify forced sex; videos depict thrill killings.

"Eat Me Alive" from *Judas Priest's* double platinum album (2 million copies sold) "Defenders of the Faith" depicts forcing oral sex at gunpoint.

Motley Crue, a heavy metal band increasingly popular with young teens, sings this in "Live Wire":

I'll either break her face
Or take down her legs
Get my ways at will
Go for the throat, never let loose.
Going in for the kill.

Or consider this from "Too Young to Fall in Love" from "Shout at the Devil":

Not a woman, but a whore
I can taste the hate
Well, now I'm killing you
Watching your face turning blue

Twisted Sister, a group often in the Top 40, has these lyrics on their "Under the Blade" album:

Your hands are tied,

Your legs are strapped.
You're going under the blade.

My 11-year-old bought Prince's 10-million-seller "Purple Rain" album because she heard an innocuous song, "Let's Go Crazy," on the radio. But once we got our purchase home, we were also treated to "Darling Nikki." The song describes "Nikki" as "a sex fiend," who spends her time "in a hotel lobby, masturbating."

Another example of Prince's work comes in the song "Sister" from the "Dirty Mind" album. The lyrics describe a 16-year old boy making love to his "lovely and loose" sister. The song concludes that "incest is everything it's said to be."

I feel that these songs, and others like them, are inappropriate for my children. Yet I find it very difficult to protect them from their twisted themes.

Studies indicate that the listening, buying and viewing audience for music is growing younger. To those who say, "Just turn it off," I submit that it is unrealistic to believe parents can control everything a child listens to.

It's time to remember that radio stations are licensed to broadcast "in the public interest," using a precious natural resource that belongs to all of us. And it isn't just radio anymore. Music videos, which are used to sell records to kids, come into our homes via broadcast TV and via cable on MTV, a 24-hour music channel, reaching 26 million homes.

Graphic sex, sadomasochism and violence, particularly toward women, are rampant on MTV. Its executives need to respond to the public outcry and curb the excesses, especially since MTV is an industry trend-setter. Jay Durbin, a music video director, has been quoted as saying he doesn't let his young children watch MTV because of the "incredible sadism."

Thomas Radechi of the National Coalition on Television Violence warns that more than half of music videos are violent. For example:

- *Def Leppard's* video "Photograph" shows the strangling of a Marilyn Monroe look-alike, and ends with her body wrapped in barbed wire.
- *Twisted Sister's* "We're Not Going to Take It Anymore" shows a son destroying his father, smashing him with doors, dragging by the hair and eventually blasting him through a plate-glass window.
- Billy Idol's "Dancing With Myself" has a naked woman struggling in chains behind a transparent sheet.
- *The Jacksons's* "Torture" shows women whipping skeletons and attacking men with claws and swords. Images of devil worship abound.
- *Van Halen's* "Hot For Teacher" features a schoolteacher doing a striptease on top of desks while elementary schoolboys ogle at her. When my 8-year-old asked me, "Why is the teacher taking off her clothes in school," I started paying attention to the videos

my children watch.

Children process reality differently from adults, a fact we too often forget. These images have powerful and terrifying effects on young minds.

In another disconcerting development, some rock artists promote and glorify suicide. Ozzy Osbourne sings "Suicide Solution"; *Blue Oyster Cult* sings "Don't Fear the Reaper"; *AC/DC* sings "Shoot to Thrill." Every year half a million teenagers attempt suicide. More than 6,000 succeed. Yet too many of the executives of the rock record industry apparently don't care.

No one should want a return to Victorian hypocrisy about sex. It was repressive at worst and unrealistic at best. But now the pendulum has swung too far toward the hedonistic and materialistic philosophy of: If it feels good, do it; if you want it, take it.

The time has come for concerned parents and consumers to demand a choice. Recently, 19 record companies offered to apply a warning label to albums containing explicit sexual material. However, each company would have its own standard as to what lyrics warranted a label. The effect in the marketplace would be to confuse the consumer.

The Parents Music Resource Center has asked the record executives to create an industrywide uniform standard defining what constitutes explicit and violent material. We of the PMRC are not trying to ban any songs, and we oppose censorship or government regulation. Instead, we believe that the music industry itself and its media outlets should voluntarily cut down on violent and sexually explicit material.

We have proposed a rating system for records, tapes and videos that the industry could administer itself.

The national PTA (National Congress of Parents and Teachers) has also been calling for records to be rated. And some responsible voices within the industry have called for restraint. George David Weiss, president of the Songwriters Guild of America, called for the music industry to tone down. "There is enough violence without glorifying it in music aimed at youngsters," he wrote in Billboard.

Even Sting, formerly of the rock group *The Police*, is on record as saying "to write pornography is to display a lack of imagination."

On Sept. 19, the Senate Commerce Committee will hold hearings on pornographic rock music.

That's the good news. The bad news is that most purveyors of porno rock think they can get by with anything by simply accusing their critics of advocating censorship.

To market explicit sex and graphic and sadistic violence to an audience of preteens and teens is a secondary form of child abuse. A society whose mass media peddles these themes challenged is abdicating its responsibility to an entire generation of young Americans. I believe in the First Amendment, but freedom always involves responsibilities.

It's not easy being a parent these days, but it's even tougher being a kid. It's about time the record industry gave us all a break.

Tipper Gore, a founder of the Parents Music Resource Center, is the mother of four, ages 2 to 11. She is married to Sen. Albert Gore Jr. (D-Tenn.). "Live Wire" and "Too Young to Fall In Love" lyrics © 1982 Warner Tamerlane Publishing Corp. and Motley Crue Publishing. "Under the Blade" lyrics used with permission of Snidest Music Co. Inc. and Zomba Enterprises.

UNDER THE BLADE

Words and Music by D. Snider

A glint of steel
A flash of light
You know you're not going home tonight
Be it jack or switch
Doctor's or mind
Nowhere to run, everywhere you'll find
You can't escape
From the bed you've made
When your time has come,
You'll accept the blade!

You're cornered in the alley way
You know you're all alone
You know it's gonna end this way
The chill goes to the bone
Now here it comes that glistening light
It goes into your side
The blackness comes
Tonight's the night
The blade is gonna ride

CHORUS:
Cause you're under the blade
Oh, you're under the blade

It's not another party head
This time you cannot rise
Your hands are tied,

Your legs are strapped
A light shines in your eyes
You faintly see a razor's edge
You open your mouth to cry
You know you can't
It's over now
The blade is gonna ride

CHORUS

You've tried to make it to the front
You're pinned against the side
A monster sands before you now
Its mouth is open wide
The lights go on, the night explodes
It tears into your mind
When the night does end,
You'll come again,
The blade is gonna ride

CHORUS

[From the Rolling Stones [sic] , Sept. 12, 1985]
**FUROR OVER ROCK LYRICS INTENSIFIES -- SENATE MAY HOLD HEARINGS
IN SEPTEMBER
(By Robert Love)
The Filthy Fifteen**

Artist and song	Rating
Judas Priest, "Eat Me Alive"	X
Motley Crue, "Bastard"	V
Prince, "Darling Nikki"	X
Sheena Easton, "Sugar Walls"	X
W.A.S.P., "(Animal) Fuck Like a Beast"	X
Mercyful Fate, "Into the Coven"	O
Vanity, "Strap On Robby Baby"	V
Def Leppard, "High 'n' Dry"	D/A

- *Twisted Sister*, "We're Not Gonna Take It"   V
- Madonna, "Dress You Up"   X
- Cyndi Lauper, "She Bop"   X
- *AC/DC*, "Let Me Put My Love Into You   X
- *Black Sabbath*, "Trashed"   D/A
- *Mary Jane Girls*, "My House"   X
- *Venom*, "Possessed"   O

A small group of well connected Washington women is spearheading the most serious protest against rock lyrics since Spiro Agnew's 1971 crusade to rid popular music of drug references. This time the primary targets are the heavy breathing hits of Prince and Madonna and the "sadomasochistic" messages of heavy metal groups like *Mötley Crüe* and *Judas Priest*. The Parents Music Resource Center (PMRC), which includes the wives of Treasury Secretary James Baker and Democratic Senator Albert Gore of Tennessee, wields sufficient political clout to have already persuaded the U.S. Senate Commerce Committee to tentatively schedule hearings on the subject for September 19th.

The PMRC wants the music industry to voluntarily institute standardized ratings, similar to movie ratings, for records, tapes and videos. Songs with sexually explicit or profane lyrics would receive an X; those that advocate the use of drugs or alcohol would receive a D/A; those that refer to the occult would receive an O; and those that glorify violence would receive a V. Also on the group's agenda is a demand that printed lyrics be available so that parents can look at them prior to purchasing an accord. In addition, record labels, distributors and broadcasters are being pressured to "exhibit voluntary restraint" in promoting what the groups calls "pornographic" and violent material.

"We're not censors," says Tipper Gore, 37, a cofounder of the five member PMRC and the mother of four young children. "We want a tool from the industry that is peddling this stuff to children, a consumer tool with which parents can make an informed decision on what to buy. What we're talking about is a sick new strain of rock music glorifying everything from forced sex to bondage to rape." Cited as particularly offensive examples are Prince's "Darling Nikki" ("I met her in a hotel lobby/Masturbating with a magazine") and *Judas Priest's* "Eat Me Alive," a song Gore says is about "oral sex at gunpoint."
In an attempt to forestall legislative action, recording

industry has been meeting privately to discuss preventive strategies. When contacted, chief executives at the major labels have refused to comment. But Stanley Gortikov, president of the Recording Industry Association of America (RIAA), has met with executives of nineteen labels, and in an August 5th letter to PMRC president Pam Howar, he presented the record industry's position. The PMRC's requests, Gortikov wrote, "involve complications that would make compliance impossible." Publishers, he explained, not record companies, own the rights to print lyrics. In addition, a label never has full control over the packaging or display of recordings or over the way its artists present themselves in performance or on video. A rating system that requires four or five categories, Gortikov wrote, would be "totally impractical."

Instead, the RIAA members would agree to "individually apply a printed inscription on packaging of future recording releases to identify blatant, explicit lyric content in order to inform those concerned parents and children. An industry wide text will be developed and used." The labels, through the RIAA will work with the PMRC to finalize the sticker's language, but Gortikov's letter offers one suggestion: "Parental guidance: Explicit lyrics." Use of the sticker would be detrimented   on a company by company basis.

This practice - applied most recently for *Eurythmics'* 1984 soundtrack album and Marvin Gaye's Dream of a Lifetime - doesn't seem to satisfy the PMRC. "I don't think that add the problem," says Gore. "We want an industry wide standard created by the industry. If you're going to leave it up to the individual record companies, just leave the mess the way it is."

Though rock lyrics have come under attack in the past, the PMRC's crusade has garnered an unusual amount of attention. As Gortikov wrote in a confidential letter to record companies, "I cannot escape continuing dialogue with the PMRC group, particularly in view of its Washington links."

The "Washington wives," as they have become known, had met with Edward Fritts, president of the National Association of Broadcasters (NAB), after his wife attended a lecture given by the group. Fritts acted with urgency, requesting that forty five record labels send lyric sheets with new releases to all radio stations to aid program directors in their choices. He also sent warning letters to 806 station owners, enclosing the lyrics to "Darling Nikki" and another Prince composition, Sheena Easton's "Sugar Walls," a song with thinly veiled references to female arousal.

"What we've got is a group of well connected parents who are raising this issue to the level of national public debate," said Fritts. "If the industry does not voluntarily respond, the PMRC would be prepared and in a position to propose legislation which would restrain the industry, which we are against."

Since Federal Communications Commission (FCC) guidelines already determine the acceptability of what may go on the air, many in the broadcasting industry considered Fritts' actions to be alarmist. As Charlie Kendall, program director of WNEW FM in New York, remarked, "We know what the lyrics are to the songs we play, and I know what my community can take. There is always gonna be an element that doesn't like rock k roll But as long as I keep it clean and within FCC guidelines, I say, 'Fuck 'em.' "

The PMRC's primary objective, a standardized record rating system, similar to the one instituted in 1968 by the Motion Picture Association of America (MPAA), has been consistently dismissed by the record companies as impractical and ultimately ineffective.

WE'RE NOT GONNA TAKE IT
Words and music by D. Snider

CHORUS:
We're not gonna take it
No, we ain't gonna take it
We're not gonna take it anymore

We've got the right to choose and
There ain't no way we'll lose it
This is our life; this is our song
We'll fight the powers that be just
Don't pick our destiny 'cause
You don't know us, you don't belong

CHORUS

Oh you're so condescending
Your gall is never ending
We don't want nothin', not a thing,
    from you
Your life is trite and jaded
Boring and confiscated
If that's your best, your best won't do

RELEASE:
OH.....................
OH....................
We're right/Yeah
We're free/Yeah
We'll fight/Yeah
You'll see/Yeah

CHORUS (TWICE)

                              UNITED WAY OF AMERICA,
                    Alexandria, VA, August 26, 1985.

        Ms. SHARI FRIEDMAN,
        Director of Video Administration,
        Atlantic Records, New York, NY.

        DEAR MS. FRIEDMAN:

        I am writing to request the use of portions of *Twisted
        Sister's* music video "We're Not Gonna Take It" in a non
        commercial television program   we are producing on the
        Changing American Family.

        Our program   is divided into segments on the progressive
        stages of family development; Love and Marriage, Children,
        Teenagers, Parents and the Elderly. The clips from the
        Twisted Sister video would be used to introduce the
        Teenagers segment in the program   . We hope that the

video's introduction with the demanding father will be a
light hearted way of talking about communication with
teenagers.

The show will be distributed to local United Ways across
the country who will in turn broadcast the program   on
their local stations. This would make it difficult when and
where the program   would be aired. We would of course
provide a "super" crediting Atlantic. The 3/4 inch format
would be preferable.

Please contact me at United Way if you have any questions
or need any additional information about our request.
Thank you for your consideration.

Sincerely,
HUGH DRESCHER,
Associate Producer.
United Way Productions.

————————◆——◇——◆————————

FREEFALL TALENT GROUP,
FREEFALL PRESENTATIONS, LTD.,
Syosset, NY, September 4 1985.

MR. HUGH DRESCHER,
United Way of America,,   Alexandria, VA.

DEAR HUGH: This letter is to confirm the use of the clips
from the *Twisted Sister* video "We're Not Gonna Take It"
for your program   , as long as it is for non commercial
use only. We would also like to request a final copy. Also
the "super" that you provide must credit Mary Callner not
Atlantic.

Best Regards,
MARK PUMA.

The CHAIRMAN. The next witness is Mrs. Millie Waterman, the National PTA vice president for legislative activity.

Ms. Waterman, thank you very much for being here.

Please proceed.

STATEMENT OF MILLIE WATERMAN, NATIONAL PTA VICE PRESIDENT FOR LEGISLATIVE ACTIVITIY, MENTOR, OH, ACCOMPANIED BY ARNOLD FEGE, DIRECTOR, GOVERNMENTAL RELATIONS

Mrs. WATERMAN. Thank you, Senator.

I have accompanying me Mr. Arnold Fege, director of governmental relations for the National PTA. I ask that he sit up here with me.

Mr. Chairman, members of the Subcommittee on Communications, I thank you for this opportunity to address the issue of record and cassette lyric labeling . I am Millie Waterman, vice president for legislative activity for the National PTA, the Nation's largest volunteer child advocacy association comprising 5.6 million members in over 25,000 local units in 50 State congresses, the District of Columbia and Europe. The National PTA is a non-profit organization interested in the protection of health, education, and welfare of children and youth.

Throughout the history of recorded music there have been complaints about the contents of some songs. The outcry over music lyrics began to rise with the introduction of rock and roll more than 30 years ago.

Senator GORE. Mr. Chairman, I am having trouble hearing the witness.

The CHAIRMAN. If you would withhold, Ms. Waterman, I want to apologize for the noise. If the officer could keep the door closed, I would very much appreciate it.
Please continue.

Mrs. WATERMAN. Thank you, Mr. Chairman.

Throughout the history of recorded music, there have been complaints about the contents of some songs. The outcry over music lyrics began to rise with the introduction of rock and roll. While parents and others interested in the wellbeing of children have continued to voice their concerns, the recording industry took no action to address this current concern until August of 1985.

Briefly, the problem is that there are many songs which include lyrics that may not be appropriate for young children or that send messages that may be dangerous to individuals or society. Some examples of songs that might be inappropriate for children are those that contain profane language, sexual references, vulgarity or violence. Those that could be dangerous to individuals or society include songs that promote suicide, practice of the occult, rape, incest, murder or bondage, among others.

Until now, no one has suggested a reasonable solution to the problem. By reasonable, we mean a solution that would not involve any form of censorship but would protect consumers from exposure to materials they feel may be harmful to themselves or children. Until 1984, no specific proposals were made or acted upon by either the public or the industry, at least none that we know of, that did not involve censorship.

In June of 1984, the National PTA's convention body, representing the 5.6 million members of the PTA, adopted a resolution which points out that an unsuspecting public may buy records, tapes and cassettes which contain explicit language, sexual references and inferences to situations not commonly recommended for all age groups. Further, it addressed the fact that there is currently no rating system in use for evaluating the content of recordings, nor any markings on jackets or covers to indicate the content. The resolution calls on the PTA to encourage recording companies to consider the explicit contents of some songs and their responsibility to an unsuspecting public. It also calls for recording companies to label record, tape and cassette covers and indicate the nature of the questionable content.

In October of 1984 the president of the National PTA sent a letter to 30 record companies and the Recording Industry Association of America explaining the resolution and suggesting that the industry convene a panel of consumer, industry and recording artist representatives to establish standards that all record companies could apply to determine which recordings need to bear a warning label.

Because our proposal to establish standards has been met with misunderstanding and confusion in the music industry, I would like to clarify it for this committee. We are not suggesting that the panel review every new song and rate it accordingly. We are suggesting that the panel produce written guidelines that each record company can follow to evaluate its own products.

The need for such standards was made clear in a response sent to the National PTA by the Recording Industry president, Stanley Gortikov on November 16, 1984, which said, "There are wide variations, company to company, within our industry in respect to artists, contractual relationships, marketing considerations and product services." With such different practices among companies, different standards might be applied to labeling   records which would only confuse the consumers and therefore provide minimal benefits.

In May of 1985 the president of the National PTA invited the presidents or representatives of 62 record companies and the Recording Industry to meet with PTA representatives at a luncheon in New York City which was scheduled for May 30. Only seven companies replied, and all declined to attend. However, three companies did offer to meet with the PTA privately to discuss the issues involved. Due to scheduling conflicts, those meetings have not yet been arranged.

In August of 1985 the Recording Industry announced that it had received agreement from 19 record companies to label recordings they deemed appropriate with a warning of some kind. The suggested wording offered was "Parental Guidance: Explicit Lyrics."

We view this as a very positive step by the music industry. It demonstrates that the industry finally recognizes there is a serious problem that affects millions of music consumers and that the problem must be addressed.

Our concern is that the industry's proposal does not define what explicit lyrics are. What is explicit to one company may be acceptable to another. In addition, it does not address the use of dangerous lyrical themes, such as the promotion of drug and alcohol use or the committing of crimes.

While a "Parental Guidance" warning would provide some relief, it does not adequately solve the entire problem, which is that music consumers have no way of knowing exactly what they are getting until they take a recording home and play it.

Together with the Parents' Music Resource Center , the National PTA is proposing that the entire music industry agree upon an appropriate symbol that would be used to designate recordings containing explicit sexual language, violence, profanity, the occult and glorification of drugs and alcohol. We are suggesting that the letter "R" be used because it is familiar to consumers as a warning that material may be inappropriate for young people or sensitive adults as part of the movie rating system. "R" would not suggest restriction. It would be used only as an alert to consumers.

Such a label would need to be either adhered to or printed on the actual recording cover, not the cellophane wrapper. For this system to work as a means for parents to monitor the music their children are bringing into their homes, they need to see the warning, which could be removed along with a cellophane wrapping.

In addition, we recommend that the lyrics on all music recordings labeled "R" be provided in some way outside the packaging. If the lyrics could not be printed on the outside of music packages, then it might be made available in some other form at record stores for consumer review. Providing lyrics will let each individual determine for himself or herself whether an "R" recording would be appropriate for personal use. We believe that the music industry should determine the best means for providing lyrics to consumers.

In conclusion, I would like to make it clear to this committee that the National PTA would in no way encourage nor support censorship of the music industry.

Second, we are asking that the use of a warning labeling system be a voluntary one undertaken by the music industry as part of its responsibility to consumers.

And, finally, the National PTA believes it is the responsibility of parents to control the types of musical materials their children listen to in their homes. Without a warning system, parents have no way to know what they are buying for their children or what their children are buying, unless then   listen to every single recording.

We hope to continue our dialog with the industry as a whole, and individual record companies, until an agreement is reached that will satisfy all parties involved.

I thank this committee for the opportunity to testify.

The CHAIRMAN. You do not believe that under the present state of affairs sufficient information is available to parents to allow them to participate in the decision as to what is in their homes?

Mrs. WATERMAN. No, sir, there is nothing that as you buy a record or tape or cassette in most records that allows you to know what is in that, and we believe that there should be a label so that they know what they purchase.

The CHAIRMAN. Do you think it is realistic to expect parents to actually sit down and play the rock music that is going into the home?

Mrs. WATERMAN. Do I believe they should play every record?

The CHAIRMAN. Do you think it is realistic to expect that they will?

Mrs. WATERMAN. I think that when they themselves buy it, if they know what it is --

The CHAIRMAN. If a child brings a record into the home, do you think that as a practical matter the parents are going to be sitting down and listening to the record?

Mrs. WATERMAN. I think that parents want to be good parents. Right now they are blindfolded, Mr. Chairman, by when they purchase a record or a tape or a cassette they do not know what is in it, and I say take the blindfold off of those parents and let them know what they buy, and then it is their responsibility of what they play in that home.

The CHAIRMAN. Senator Hollings.

Senator HOLLINGS. I thank Ms. Waterman, Mr. Chairman, and yield my time.

The CHAIRMAN. Senator Gore.

Senator GORE. Thank you, Mr. Chairman.

I would like to note for the record that the National PTA was the first organization to make this issue a major concern. In October of 1984 you passed a resolution at your national convention requesting assistance from the record industry. Is that correct?

Mrs. WATERMAN. That is correct, Senator.

Senator GORE. As a result of that resolution, you then contacted the major record companies asking for a response to your request that they voluntarily put ratings on albums, is that right?

Mrs. WATERMAN. That is correct.

Senator GORE. How many of the major record companies responded to that letter from the National PTA?

Mrs. WATERMAN. I think I told you in my testimony, seven. Very few of them. And the meetings, of course, never came off. Seven companies replied, sir.

Senator GORE. Seven companies?

Mrs. WATERMAN. Yes.

Senator GORE. Did any of them respond favorably ?

Mrs. WATERMAN. No.

Senator GORE. None of them did?

Mrs. WATERMAN. No.

Senator GORE. You asked for a meeting with the record companies, is that right?

Mrs. WATERMAN. That is right.

Senator GORE. But that meeting has not yet occurred, is that right?

Mrs. WATERMAN. That meeting has never taken place, sir.

Senator GORE. Did you get the feeling that you were being stonewalled by the industry, or that they were resisting any effort to engage in a dialog with you?

Mrs. WATERMAN. You would have that feeling. However, 19 companies have agreed that there would be some kind of labeling, "Parental Guidance: Explicit Lyrics." So there is a movement of concern certainly if those 19 have agreed.

Senator GORE. Do you share the concern of the PMRC that if these record companies are going to voluntarily label albums and cassettes, the set of criteria governing when a label is appropriate and when it is not, should be industrywide and not just according to the different criteria of each individual company?

Mrs. WATERMAN. Senator Gore, we feel that a panel of the music industry should sit down and do the guidelines and standards so that all of them are the same. Otherwise it would not – one company would be one way, one would be the other. It needs to be uniform.

Senator GORE. Now, although there are some differences between the remedies you have suggested and those suggested by the PMRC, if I am correct, the two organizations have met and worked out a common approach that meets the concerns of both groups, is that correct?

Mrs. WATERMAN. The president of the National PTA has had a meeting with the PMRC, and we agree on three things. I felt that the agreement was on the need for labeling,   the need for lyrics to be placed so that a parent or a buyer could see what they were, and also the panel needed to be convened of the music industry, that it be voluntarily done.

Senator GORE. Well, I congratulate you for the leadership offered by the PTA in this matter. I hope you will keep it up, and will carry this message to your local chapters throughout the country.

Thank you very much for appearing.

Mrs. WATERMAN. Thank you, Senator Gore.

Senator GORE. Thank you, Mr. Chairman.

The CHAIRMAN. Senator Riegle?

Senator RIEGLE. Thank you, Mr. Chairman.

We have been involved this morning in the Banking Committee, as you may know, with the nominee for the position of head of the FDIC. We have also had the Social Security issue on the Senate floor, at least prospectively, and that has occupied myself and others of us.

I would like to ask you, Mr. Chairman – on the basis of the response, I may want to pose another question to the witness. Has an argument been advanced as to why rating systems have been and seem to be effectively used in rating motion pictures and therefore cannot as readily be adapted to records?

I mean, has there been any convincing reason presented as to why it can be done apparently with some effectiveness in that area of creative material and not as readily done in the record area?

The CHAIRMAN. There has been very little discussion of the relationship between ratings of motion pictures and ratings of records. There has been some reference to it, but very little discussion.

Senator RIEGLE. I take it that the position that has been advanced by the record spokesmen that have appeared is to the effect that full disclosure, any kind of a presenting and writing of the lyrics, when we have material that would be in this area, that would be offensive to many people, that the full disclosure is somehow seen as an invasion of rights? Is that the thrust of the argument that has been advanced?

The CHAIRMAN. I am hesitant to characterize other people's arguments. Mr. Zappa took the position that the printing of lyrics would be something that would be satisfactory to him. He thought that a rating system would be arbitrary and would falsely impugn the integrity of people in the music business.

Senator RIEGLE. Well, it seems to me that the bridge has been crossed in the motion picture business, in effect. Now, the two are not exactly the same, but I think the proposition is essentially the same.

Would it be the view of the National PTA that having taken that step with respect to motion pictures and now having a system there which seems to have met with the general acceptance by both artists and moviemakers as well as the public, that that would be an example of something that would work just as readily in the record business?
Would that be your view?

Mrs. WATERMAN. I think what we are asking for, Senator, is a rating system. You know the National PTA has been on record over the years on their concern for television violence, on their concern on movies, and we did ask for a rating system in movies. We are not asking for a rating system or label on the records restricting age. What we are asking is that that label does provide the consumer who wishes to buy or chooses not to, that he knows what is within that record. So we would not be putting age on it. But the National PTA has been on record in their protection of children and youth over nearly 90 years now in their concern on media, and we have in no way ever encouraged censorship, but we have always asked that the private industry limit themselves to knowing what is good and have a responsibility to society and children. And the National PTA in the 1984 convention took this step because they were very concerned on what their children were hearing on records and what they as a parent, when they went to buy, had no way of knowing.

Senator RIEGLE. How do you envision, or how does the National PTA envision the best way if standards are going to be established. How would you see that done?

Mrs. WATERMAN. Well, the industry is going to have to clean their own house, just to be very frank. We have asked for a voluntary panel of the music industry that they can choose their own people to set up their guidelines and their standards, and we would certainly work with them in any way that we could, and we hope that this is done.

I think there has been some concern voiced here today. I listened very intently to the artists and to the PMRC and to everyone else that has testified, and there are obviously, and on this panel also, and there has been obvious concern as to what this hearing is all about.

I think that we will come to a responsible solution to this.

Senator RIEGLE. So the PTA is not suggesting any kind of a system as to how these ratings would be done, or what they would be or what would be included or left out, but rather, that you would like to see the recording industry and the artists sit down together and develop their own methodology? Is that the idea?

You are not trying to put yourself in that standard-setting business?

Mrs. WATERMAN. Senator, I think to answer your question completely, the resolution spoke very clearly to the rating, the label that should be violence or profanity or sex or occult or drugs. The knowing what is in the package was very important to the people of that convention of which there were thousands.

Now, when you are saying adding, that we believe voluntarily, we are hoping that the music industry will set up this panel, will set up their guidelines and their standards, and that it will be pleasing to all of us who are concerned.

Senator RIEGLE. My time has expired at this point, Mr. Chairman.

The CHAIRMAN. Thank you very much, Mrs. Waterman, for your testimony and for your patience in waiting so long.

Mrs. WATERMAN. Thank you for the forum.

STATEMENTS OF DR. JOE STUESSY, UNIVERSITY OF TEXAS AT SAN ANTONIO, AND DR. PAUL KING, MEMPHIS, TN

Mr. STUESSY. Yes, sir.

Mr. Chairman, Senators and guests, thank you for allowing me to make a few remarks. I have submitted a substantial written testimony. I hope you will take the chance to read it because my 5-minute speech will be rather brief and just try to hit the main topics. Substantiation is in the written documentation.

Let me see if I can convey to you what we know from the field of music psychology about music and its interrelationship with people. I should say that I am on the music faculty of the University of Texas at San Antonio. I hold a Ph.D. in music, and have taught a course in the history of rock music for 12 years at two universities.

The first thing we know is that music affects behavior . Many children will say I listen to that stuff, but it does not affect me. In fact, Mr. Snider said exactly those words earlier today. He said, it does not affect me. We have known intuitively for centuries, and it has been proven conclusively by scientific studies in recent decades that music does affect behavior .

Music affects our moods, emotions, attitudes, and our resultant behavior . Music affects us psychologically and physiologically. This fact explains why we have choirs and organs at church, why we have bands at football games, Muzak in stores, business offices, and doctors' offices. It explains why there are military marches, discothèques, music behind movies and TV, Jazzercise, and most importantly, commercial jingles.

We know some other things about the way music interacts with people. We know that music is an aid to verbal retention. Any verbal message that you receive, you are more likely to remember if it is in a musical context.

We also know that repetition increases our preference for that which is repeated. The more we hear things, the more likely we are to internalize it and like it.

We also know that coordinated multisensory input reinforces music's message. The more senses that can be evolved in receiving a coordinated message, the more likely that message is to impact upon our conscious and subconscious.

Although this next point may seem contradictory to the previous one, it is really not, and that is that there is such a thing as exclusionary input, that is to say, input which blocks out all other inputs, thus removing distractions. We also know that exclusionary input increase the impact on the mind of the messages being received.

Today's heavy metal music is categorically different from previous forms of popular music. It contains the element of hatred, a meanness of spirit. Its principal themes are, as you have already heard, extreme violence, extreme rebellion, substance abuse, sexual promiscuity and perversion and Satanism. I know personally of no form of popular music before which has had as one of its central elements the element of hatred.

The message may be either overt or covert. In the case of the overt message, we are talking of course about a message which is being reinforced by music, something we have said increases the verbal message's impact. It is being reinforced by repetition, primary and secondary repetition; primary meaning that within the same song a given hook line is repeated as many times as 30 or 40 times in a 3 or 4 minute span; secondary repetition comes about because frequently the words are very difficult to understand. Typically, the teenager therefore will listen repetitively, over and over and over, to understand the words and frequently be able to transcribe them.

The message is reinforced by multisensory input such as the album covers, which have been discussed, the looks of the performers, their theatrics on stage, the visual representations such as MTV, volume levels, etc. And the message is reinforced in individual headphone listening, which is a type of exclusionary listening that I referred to earlier.

The message may also be covert or subliminal. Sometimes sub-audible tracks are mixed in underneath other, louder tracks. These are heard by the subconscious but not the conscious mind. Sometimes the messages are audible but are backwards, called back-masking. There is disagreement among experts regarding the effectiveness of subliminals. We need more research on that.

We hear frequently about the first amendment problem. In closing, I would say that while we must protect our first amendment freedoms, we must also protect minors from the abuse of those freedoms. The first amendment, as I understand it, is not a blank check. There are legal, constitutional limitations when we feel that the abuse or the use of a freedom negatively impacts the health of another segment of society. Use of the airwaves for pornography and immoral purposes, especially when aimed at minors, must be controlled somehow. Given the American philosophy, I think we have given the so-called creative artists a wide berth. We have given them more than the proverbial inch, and I believe they have taken more than the proverbial mile.

Somehow we must send a message to the recording and radio industry; enough is enough; you have gone too far. Parents are fighting this scourge all over the country. We plead for help from city councils, radio stations, advertisers and the record industry itself.

I hope that this committee will find a way to send a message to the industry: clean up your act or we will do it for you.

In the words of the heavy metal band, *Twisted Sister*, "we're not going to take it anymore."

Thank you.

[The statement follows]

STATEMENT OF DR. JOE STUESSY

I

A Few Brief Remarks About My Background
(Or "Who is this guy?")

I like rock and roll. I am a former professional rock musician (at the local level); about half of my rather extensive record collection is rock music. I hold a Ph.D. in music from the Eastman School of Music and am currently a Professor of Music at the University of Texas at San Antonio. I was among the first in the nation to teach a university course in the history of rock music (that was in 1973; in 1985 there are many such courses). I have taught this course at two universities (Southern Methodist University and the University of Texas at San Antonio). I have had over 3,000 students in that course over the intervening twelve years.

I full résumé is appended to this testimony if further information is desired.

II

Some Things We Know About Music and Human Behavior
(Or, "I listen to that stuff, but it doesn't affect me!")

A.   Music affects behavior. This simple fact has been known intuitively for centuries. For example, Plato's mentor, Damon, said that music can "not only arouse or allay different emotions, but also inculcate all the virtues--courage, self-restraint, and even justice."(1) Many centuries later, Martin Luther said, "Music is one of the greatest gifts that God has given us; it is divine and therefore Satan is its enemy. For with its aid, many dire temptations are overcome; the devil does not stay where music is." (2) We can probably assume that Martin Luther was not familiar with Heavy Metal!

In the twentieth century, especially in the last four decades, tons of research has been done on the interrelationship of music and human behavior . Although each study addresses slightly different aspects of this general premise, the aggregate conclusion is clear: music affects human behavior . It affects our moods, our attitudes, our emotions, and our behavior . It affects us psychologically and physiologically.

Anthropologist A. P. Merriam in his book The Anthropology of Music says, "The importance of music, as judged by the sheer ubiquity of its presence, is enormous...there is probably no other human cultural activity which is so all-pervasive and which reaches into, shapes, and often controls so much of human behavior. " (3) In his study of George Orwell's 1984, Dr. Paul Haack summarized the numerous references to music as follows: "The most striking feature of these references is the constant, blatant propagandizing and mind controlling function that the music serves." (4)

Music can make us feel relaxed, scared, patriotic, ambitious, mad, sad, happy, romantic, reverent, etc. The fact that music affects behavior   is the foundation of the entire science of music therapy, a field in which music is applied as a therpeutic   tool to modify aberrant behavior.

Think for a moment of just a few of the ways that the presence of music affects our average daily lives:

1.   Music in business offices, if properly structured, can have a positive (or negative) effect on worker efficiency. Companies such as Muzak, Inc. have done many studies which document this fact.
2.   Similarly, music in doctors' and dentists' offices is used to relax patients and calm anxieties. In some cases, music has been used as an aid in pain reduction.
3.   Music in retail establishments is used to partially sedate the shopper, making him/her more receptive to marketing stratagems.
4.   Music at sporting events is used to inspire enthusiasm for the home team (fight songs, Alma Maters, etc.).

5.   "The Star-spangled Banner" and other patriotic tunes are played on July Fourth celebrations (and other times) to inspire a feeling of pride and patriotism.

6.   Music accompanies movies and television shows and is used to affect the viewers' emotions and expectations. For example, when the camera slowly proceeds up a dark path with woods on either side, the presence of "spooky" music heightens our expectation that someone is going to jump out from behind a tree, brandishing a knife. We become nervous and apprehensive; we tighten up and hold onto our seats; our pulse and heartbeat quicken. These affects would be less likely if the music at that moment were the theme song from "I Love Lucy!"

7.   When you think about it, dancing is a rather silly-looking activity. Next time you see a dance floor filled with people, imagine the same exact scene, but without music. Kinda stupid, isn't it? Either people would be jumping spastically around for no apparent reason (fast tune), or they would be draped over each other in a near-motionless embrace (slow tune). What makes this silly behavior OK? MUSIC!

8.   Bugle calls and marches have historically been used to intensify courage on the part of men in battle. The right music prepares us to charge over that next hill, bayonets poised, ready to meet the enemy (or our own death).

9.   When we are entering church on Sunday mornings, we are greeted with the reverent sounds of an organ. Choirs sing songs of praise. The congregation sings hymns of faith. All of this is done for a reason. It reinforces and enhances our reverence, our faith, our love of God, and our determination to live letter lives.

10.   An entire industry today is based on the idea that people will put on skimpy outfits and travel miles away several times per week for the purpose of exercising and sweating. And they'll pay for the privilege! Without music, this activity is just plain hard work. With music, it's fun! Jazzercise and similar exercise-to-music activities are flourishing all over the nation.

11.   Perhaps the best example of music affecting behavior is the commercial jingle. The Sears, Penneys, Toyotas, Dr. Peppers, and Budweisers of the world spend millions annually on catchy advertising slogans set to music. I'll have more to say about that later. For now, let's assume the companies which spend hundred of thousands of dollars to get their musical jingle on a Super Bowl broadcast for a few seconds are really not stupid! They know exactly what they are doing. They know that such a message will increase the likelihood of the listeners buying their services or products. It works.

B.   Music is an aid in verbal retention. Studies (Lathom, 1970; Mann, 1979; Wintle, 1978) have shown that we can memorize and retain verbal information better if that information is presented in a short, catchy musical setting. The makers of Sesame Street certainly knew that and used it most effectively in teaching letters and numbers via their "commercials" for the letter K or the number 8. Currently a hotel chain is running a national advertising campaign in which they sing their telephone number. They are correct in thinking that it is more likely to be remembered because of the catchy rhythmic/melodic context. Once implanted, such verbal information stays with us a long time. For example, if I say, "Oh what a feeling – " I'll bet you can fill in the blank with a car manufacturer's name. You can probably even sing the tune – in rhythm! How many other jingles can you still remember from years ago? Try "Baseball, hot dogs, apple pie, and – " or "Wouldn't you like to be a – too," or "See the USA in your – " That last one is thirty years old!

C.   Repetition increases our preference for that which is repeated. Again, studies (Verveer, 1933; Mull, 1940; Meyer, 1960; Bartlett, 1969; Pantle, 1977) have shown that even if we are not favorably   impressed with a piece of music the first time we hear it, most often such pieces tend to grow on us. As we become more familiar with it, begin to understand it, and as it becomes more "'internalized" we not only find ourselves liking it more, but actually catch ourselves whistling it or singing it (subconsciously--that's important, by the way!). Think of one of your personal favorites   (whether it's Beethoven or the Beatles). Can you remember the very first time you heard it? Were you as wild about it then as you are now? Probably not. There are always a few exceptions – the piece we love on first hearing. But all of Top 40 radio is based on the premise that repetitive listening increases preference for that which is repeated.

D.   Coordinated multi-sensory input reinforces any message. Salesmen know this. If a salesman can coordinate a major presentation so that his client hears his message verbally, reads his message in printed form, sees some slides and a few graphs, etc, the impact of his message will be greater. Teachers know this. Some of the finest teaching I have seen involved a coordinated presentation with verbal, written, and visual factors all focused to teach a given concept.

E.   "Exclusionary" input also enhances the impact of a message. (This seems to conflict with item D above, but notice that important word "coordinated" in item D.) By exclusionary input, I mean single-source input which blocks out all other conflicting or distracting inputs. Would you want to give an important political speech in the middle of Grand Central Station at the 5:00 p.m. rush hour? Probably not. You simply would not have people's undivided attention. There would be too many distractions. We know that we are bombarded with aural input every minute. Even in a relatively quiet room, there may be the sound of air-conditioning systems, fluorescent lights buzzing, shoes squeaking, papers rustling, chairs scooting, not to mention the internal sounds of our own heartbeat, pulse, and respiration--plus anyone who is speaking and any music that is playing. Imagine how much more effectively our mind could concentrate on a message if most of these competing sounds were blocked out.

F.   Stimulative music, while stimulating some bodily processes, may actually sedate others. This fact is suspected, but not yet proven conclusively to my knowledge. But we do know that some things stimulate some aspects of our activites   while depressing others. For example, three or four stiff alcoholic drinks may make you the life of the party (stimulated), but at the same time you may slur your words or trip over the carpet (these and other faculties have been numbed or depressed). It is an interesting contradictory effect of some so-called "stimulants."

III
Is Heavy Metal Really Different?
(Or, "Isn't this just the same old fuddy-duddies against the same old rock and roll?")

New musical styles have typically elicited negative reactions. The waltz was considered a depraved and licentious phenomenon which should never replace the more proper minuet. Stravinsky's Rite of Spring was soundly booed at its premiere and described as primitive and animalistic. Jazz was berated as decadent and immoral music. And, of course, rock and roll was declared to be noisy and sexually provocative music from the beginning.

So here we are in 1985; again, a group of people is decrying the negative and potentially harmful affects of an abrasive musical style. Is this current debate just more of the same, or is it really something different? Is it just a matter of degree or is it a difference in kind?

Both! We all know that differences in degree can be so extreme that they become differences in kind. Zero and 120 are differences in degree on the scale; but the difference in degree is so great that we perceive them as opposites ("cold" and "hot" respectively). When we drive a car a 90 mph, that is just a difference in degree from 10 mph; but we call one speed "slow" and the other one "fast." As we move along any continuum, we reach a point where the characteristics of one end are categorically different (opposite) from the characteristics of the other end.

Rock and roll has always been a rebellious music. It has often had sexual overtones. In fact the terms "rocking" and "rolling" were euphemisms for sexual intercourse in rhythm and blues music (the style from which rock emerged).

So, is heavy metal just a difference in degree from Elvis, Little Richard, Jerry Lee Lewis, etc.? Or is it categorically different? Greg Stevens (former Program Director for San Antonio heavy metal station KISS-FM) says, "It's the typical rebellion of rock. It's just the modern day version of that same rebel in black leather that Elvis Presley expressed in the '50s." (5)

But why, then, do so many reasonable, fairly "hip" people (even staunch rock and roll fans) sense that there is something really different about heavy metal--that it is more than a simple extension of good old rock and roll? Dwight Silverman, a writer for the San Antonio Light, may have put his finger on it best when he wrote, "Heavy Metal rock 'n' roll is a different beast from the music that ruled the late '60s and early '70s, the music that was supposed to bring a generation together. Heavy metal is a mean-spirited music. In it, women are abused, parents are objects of derision and scorn and violence, education is a foolish waste of time. Rock 'n' roll always has been a music of rebellion and frustration, but never of hatred." (6)

Hatred. A mean-spirited music. To my knowledge, their has never been a popular style of music which had as a central characteristic the element of hate. This is something new and different. Its seeds may be found in the mid-1960s. It was nourished and developed in the late '60s and throughout the '70s. It has burst upon the 1980s as a full-grown force.

To understand the difference between earlier rock and current heavy metal, it is useful to make direct comparisons of songs from each period which address similar topics. For example, compare two songs about school and the educational experience. In the late 1950s, Chuck Berry released a song called "School Days." In it, he describes a typical school day ("the teacher is teaching the Golden Rule," and "Your studyin' hard and hopin' to pass"). Note particularly the reference to school dismissal: "Soon as 3 o'clock rolls around, you finally lay your burden down." He goes on to say that our typical teenager leaves school, goes to a "juke joint," listens to some rock and roll and dances. Now compare that to "School Daze" by *WASP*. They refer to school as "a textbook madhouse," "a juvenile jail," "a blackboard jungle," and " a homework hellhouse." And what do they say about school dismissal? "Tick, tock, 3 o'clock, I'm sitting' here counting off the days; a fire bell ringing hell and I'd sure love to see it blaze--Burn it down! [screamed]." (8)

Or consider two songs, one from the early '60s and one from the early '80s, which are almost like teen anthems. Bob Dylan's "Blowin' in the Wind" advised the younger generation of their goals in creating a better world. "...how many times must the cannon balls fly before they're forever banned?" and "...how many years can some people exist before they're allowed to be free?" (9) The song speaks of love of fellow man, peace, and racial equality. Again, contrast that with Ozzy Osbourne's "Rock 'n' Roll Rebel." After many lines of deprecation of "them" (parents and other authority figures), Ozzy threatens, "Do what you will to try and make me conform, but I'll make you wish that you had never been born; cause I'm a rock 'n' roll rebel and I'll do as I please." (10)

Finally, compare two songs which refer to the age-old parent-child conflict within the family. *The Coasters* ('50s) sang a song called "Yakety-yak." Each verse recites typical parental commands (e.g., "you just put on your coat and hat, and walk yourself to the laundry mat; and when you finish doin' that, bring in the dog and put out the cat.") (11). The hook line is "Yakety yak--don't talk back." The message seems to say to the teenager, "yeh, I understand your problem." But it never suggests violence or open rebellion, and certainly not hatred. But the song's 1980s counterpart might be a song by *Twisted Sister* called "We're Not Gonna Take It." They have a different message for parents:

> "Oh you're so condescending; your gall is never-ending;
> We don't want nothin', not a thing from you.
> Your life is trite and jaded, boring and confiscated;
> If that's your best, your best won't do.
>
> Oh, Oh, we're right, we're free, we'll fight, you'll see!
>
> We're not gonna take it; no, we're not gonna take it;
> We're not gonna take it anymore [screamed: Just you try and make us!]"(12)

The accompanying video shows a teenager who is transformed into *Twisted Sister* lead singer D. Snider, who proceeds to attack the teen's father.

We could continue, but perhaps the message is clear. The current heavy metal is categorically different from the earlier rock 'n' roll. Even if we could agree that the difference is merely one of degree, we must conclude that the degree of difference is so great as to be a difference in kind.

IV
Is There, Then, Reason To Think That Heavy Metal Can Affect Human Behavior?
(Or, "So what!")

A.   Most of the successful heavy metal music projects one or more of the following basic themes:

a.   extreme rebellion
b.   extreme violence
c.   substance abuse
d.   sexual promiscuity/perversion (including homosexuality, bisexuality, sado-masochism, necrophilia, etc.)
e.   Satanism

Testimony by Mr. Jeff Ling will provide more than ample evidence of heavy metal's projection of these themes.

These five basic themes are projected by overt messages. Let us now see how the music works to affect behavior, as based upon the principals discussed in section II above.

1.   Remember that music reinforces verbal retention. The messages of commercial advertisers are more easily retained in our memory because they are set into a musical context. If you can still recall "See the USA in your Chevrolet," (assuming you are old enough to remember it from 30 years ago!), we can conclude that the message was firmly stored in your subconscious for later retrieval. Similarly, heavy metal lyrics, especially "hook lines" like "We're not gonna take it anymore," or "Lick it up," or "Eat me alive" are going to be stored in the current teenager's subconscious. The teen may or may not act upon this information, but we can be relatively certain that the mind has stored it away for future reference.

2.   We said that repetition reinforces the message. With heavy metal, there are two kinds of repetition. I refer to them as primary and secondary repetition. Primary repetition is integral to a given song per se. Catchy hook lines are repeated over and over within a song. For example, in "Lick It Up" by *KISS*, the hook line (the title) is repeated thirty times in this four-minute piece. That's an average of one time every eight seconds. If I were to repeat a short message to you thirty times in the next four minutes, I'll bet you would remember it for quite a while! And remember that as an additional retention aid, the hook line is set to music. The hook line (and title) "Eat Me Alive" by *Judas Priest* is repeated eighteen times in 3½ minutes. *Twisted Sister's* line "We're Not Gonna Take It" is repeated 24 times in three minutes and forty seconds. Let's face it: you never

beard "See the USA in your Chevrolet" that often, yet your subconscious can still retrieve it.

Secondary repetition is more elusive. Adults often have difficulty understanding the words to heavy metal rock songs. And guess what! So do the kids. But they are determined to grasp every profound nugget of wisdom their heavy metal mentors spew forth! So they put on headphones and play the songs over and over, for hours if necessary, in order to decipher the words. Often they write them down in notebooks. In the process, more repetitive listening reinforces the message even further.

3.   Recall that coordinated multi-sensory input also reinforces messages. The message of heavy metal music bombards our senses from every direction. The album covers display Satanic symbols, portrayals of violence, open and free sex, and angry defiance. The names of the groups, the song titles, the names of the performers (e.g., Blackie Lawless), words of the songs, and the liner notes reinforce one or more of the basic themes. The facial expressions, the hair, the clothes all contribute to the same messages. The videos and the histrionic antics of the live stage performance add a strong visual impact. The light shows, the smoke devices, and the sheer volume add impact. One can literally feel the music at a live concert, as the rib cage vibrates with every beat. Heavy metal is a media expert's dream-come-true. If the youngsters at the live concert happen to be smoking marijuana (as a great many do), please add the senses of smell and taste. That about rounds out all five senses: you hear it, you see it, you feel it, you taste it, and you smell it!

4.   As mentioned earlier, "exclusionary" input enhances the impact of a message. The phenomenon usually results from the parents' yelling for the teenager to "turn it down," or "turn it off," or "go to your room to listen to that stuff!" Often, they do just that. They go to their rooms, and put on the headphones (volume up, of course). When that happens, exclusionary input takes over. Now all distracting or competing input is blocked out. The heavy metal becomes the sole point of concentration. Now the teenager's mind need not be distracted by dishes rattling in the kitchen, little brother watching sitcoms in the next room, the dog barking, or even the telephone ringing (now that's a problem!). Literally, they can't hear it thunder! But heavy metal now has a direct, unfettered freeway straight into the mind.

5.   Finally, we suspect that stimulative music (heavy metal surely qualifies) stimulate certain bodily functions while actually sedating others (much like alcohol). The simplicity, the repetitive beat, and the uniformity of timbre and dynamics may contribute to a lowered level of consciousness. This may be why parents report that when their youngsters sit in apparent head-phoned reverence while listening to music, they seem almost trancelike. If this is true (and we must admit that phenomenon has yet to be scientifically substantiated to my knowledge), it would imply that while in such a state, the listener has a greater susceptability to suggestion. When our conscious mind "dozes," our subconscious is left with its guard down and rather indiscriminately accepts all input. Further study of this possible phenomenon is needed.

C.   There has been much speculation about the use of covert messages (subliminals) in heavy metal music. It is said that two kinds of subliminals exist.

1.   Sub-audibles (forward messages). Most contemporary rock recordings consist multiple tracks (at least 16) which are mixed together at various levels. It is possible that one such track could contain a verbal message (Satanic, sexual, or anything). This track could be mixed in at such a low level that the other tracks easily cover it. If heard by itself, it would be audible; but mixed underneath fifteen or more other tracks, it is inaudible to the conscious mind. But, as the theory goes, the subconscious mind soaks up (and stores) all input. This type of message to the subconscious is one type of "subliminal" message. (A variant on this technique is to record the message normally, and then mix it in at high speed. Again, the conscious mind misses it; but does the subconscious?)

2.   Backmasking (backwards messages). Some messages are presented to the listener backwards. While listening to a normal forward message (often somewhat nonsensical), one is simultaneously being treated to a backwards message (in other words, the lyric sounds like one set of words going forward, and a different set of words going backwards). Some experts believe that while the conscious mind is absorbing the forward lyric, the subconscious is working overtime to decipher the backwards message. Of course by spinning the record backwards (or by tape manipulation), the conscious mind gets a chance to hear the message too!

There has been much controversy about subliminals (both forward sub-audibles and backmasking). Several countries (e.g. Belgium, Great Britain) have banned the use of subliminals. The National Association of Broadcasters issued a rule forbidding its members' use of subliminals.13 The FCC says that the use of subliminals in advertising is "inconsistent with the obligations of the license...[and] contrary to the public interest." They continued, "Whether effective or not, such broadcasts are clearly intended to be deceptive." (14) A United Nations study concluded that "the cultural implications of subliminal indoctrination is a major threat to human rights throughout the world." (15) Aryeh Neier (formerly executive director of the ACLU[)] said, "People have a right to go about their business without being subjected to manipulation they don't even know about." (16) Olivia Goodkin, an attorney, said in testimony before the U.S. House Committee on Transportation, Aviation, and Materials (hearing on subliminal communication technology) that "undisclosed subliminal communication poses an unusual kind of captivity... since the audience cannot avert its eyes or shut its ears or retreat to private places if it does not even know that the communication is taking place." (17) Subliminals are, at the very least, an invasion of privacy.

Again, more research is needed to determine the actual extent to which are used and the extent to which they influence the listener.

V
SUMMARY

A. We know that music affects behavior.   Anyone who says, "I listen to heavy metal, hut it doesn't affect me" is simply wrong. Granted, it affects different people to different degrees and in different ways. The healthy, stable, mature personality may, in fact, be minimally affected by heavy metal. But many, especially teenagers and pre-teens, are still shaping their self-identities. They are malleable, beset by internal and external conflicts about authority (especially parents), drugs, sex, theology, education, etc. They are in the process of defining who and what they are. At such a time, heavy metal's influence can be significant.
What should we as a society do to protect minors from the negative, often outright pornographic influences of heavy metal? What can we do? Parental awareness (and hopefully resultant counter-influences) is a desirable first step. But this can be ineffective. By his very nature, the teenager often does exactly the opposite of what the parent suggests. Anything stronger than suggestion (such as outright control) often leads to full-scale rebellion (especially if heavy metal music has already pounded its message in).

Can society in general (through its elected officials) help? Maybe. But what about the first amendment to the Constitution? While we must protect our first amendment freedoms, we must also protect minors from the abuse of those freedoms. The first amendment is not a blank check! There are legal, constitutional limitations. Any freedom carries responsibilities. Use of the public airwaves for pornographic and immoral purposes, especially when aimed at minors, must be controlled somehow. Open retail availability of pornographic records should be treated just as any other retail of pornography (books, "adult" movies, etc.).
Given the American philosophy, we have awarded the so-called creative artist a wide berth. We have given them more than the proverbial inch; and they have taken more than the proverbial mile. Indeed, our prior liberality may go a long way toward explaining how we have arrived at this unhappy point today.

Somehow we must send a strong message to the recording and radio industries: "Enough is enough! You have gone too far." Parents, teachers, ministers, and civic leaders are fighting this scourge all over the country. We plead for help from city councils, radio stations, advertisers, retailers, and the record industry itself!

I hope that this committee will find a way to send a message to the industry: "Clean up your act or we will do it for you!" In the words of *Twisted Sister*, "We're not gonna take it anymore!"

NOTES

(1) Donald A. Hodges, The Significance of Music, an unpublished manuscript, p. 93.
(2) Ibid.
(3) A. P. Merriam, The Anthropology of Music (Chicago: Northwestern University Press, 1964), p. 218.
(4) Hodges, op. cit., p. 94.

(5) (unsigned article), "A loud mix of rebellion, energy make heavy metal," San Antonio Light, Sunday, March 10, 1985, page A16.
(6) Dwight Silverman, "Drugs, violence steal the show," San Antonio Light, Sunday, March 10, 1985, page A16.
(7) "School Days" by Chuck Berry, Inc.; published by ARC Music Corporation (BMI).
(8) "School Daze" by Blackie Lawless; published by Zomba Enterprises, Inc.
(9) "Blowin' in the Wind" by Bob Dylan, Writings and Drawings, © 1973 Bob Dylan; published by Alfred A. Knopf, Inc., New York, page 33.
(10) "Rock 'n' Roll Rebel" by Ozzy Osbourne © 1983 Nymph Music, Inc. (BMI).
(11) "Yakety Yak" by Jerry Leiber and Mike Stoller; published by Tiger (BMI).
(12) "We're Not Gonna Take It" by D. Snider, © 1984 Snidest Music Co. (ASCAP).
(13) Dan and Steve Peters, Rock's Hidden Persuader: The Truth About Backmasking (Minneapolis: Bethany House Publishers, 1985), page 17.
(14) Ibid., page 19.
(15) Ibid.
(16) Ibid., page 73.
(17) Ibid., page 111.

The CHAIRMAN. Thank you, sir.

Dr. King.

Dr. KING. My name is Paul King, and I am a child and adolescent psychiatrist. I treat kids with serious drug problems. I have been treating adolescents for 9 years.

Senator RIEGLE. Excuse me. Could you pull the mike a little closer?

Dr. KING. I have been treating adolescents for over 9 years, and have formerly also been a New York City high school teacher. So I have been working with teenagers for over 14 years now.

The kids that I treat, some are delinquent, some are suicidal, others are violent, even homicidal. Many are sexually promiscuous. Nearly all of my patients worship heavy metal music.

My comments are not really my own but reflect what I have learned from the kids that I see each and every day in my practice. I would like to talk about two points. One is to answer the question about whether music influences young people or not, and the other is the issue about parents and the type of guidance, and what is the nature of sufficient guidance for parents in this issue.

With the aid of sophisticated marketing techniques, entertainers are elevated to the role of deities, to be worshipped by youth as if they are gods. Long hours are spent listening to heavy metal rock music, with some performers portraying themselves as charismatic leaders. The young person may then identify with the words of the song, "You've given me a new belief." "Belief" has religious connotations, "And soon the world will love you sweet leaf." Sweet Leaf, by *Black Sabbath*, Warner Brothers Records. Adolescents tell me sweet leaf refers to marijuana.

Rebellion and hate are common themes. "Children of the Grave," by *Black Sabbath*: "Revolution on their minds/The children march/Against the world they have to live in/Oh the hate that's in their hearts." The group leader is a preacher, and the young person who becomes involved with the lyrics develops a belief system, internalizes a belief system based on those lyrics.

Heavy metal refers to a type of music that was first developed in England. The music is loud and powerful, with most of the strength coming from electric guitars. The makeup or facial expressions are either hateful or demonic or have symbols and costumes representing power, which is the basic core issue. Examples, facial painting in what Kiss used to wear, tatoos of snarling animals, black leather, chains, motorcycles. We have seen examples. Members of the group *Motley Crue* wear pentagrams.

Verbal overtures are extremely philosophical. Let me give you a few examples. "The Number of the Beast" by Iron Maiden, which is Zomba Enterprises, and it goes "Woe to you, oh earth and sea./ For the Devil sends the beast with wrath,/because he knows the time is short./Let him who has understanding reckon/the number of the beast,/for it is a human number./His number is 666." The 666 refers to the Beast from Revelations.

Young people "Shout at the Devil." It has a prologue. It is not even the music, it is a prologue with a very clear message, the idea so that that could be clearly listened to. "In the beginning/ the court of good always overpowered/the evils of all man's sins./But in time, the nations grew weak,/ and our cities fell to slums/while evil stood strong./In the dust of hell/lurked the blackest of hates./ For he who men fear awaits you."

"But now, many many lifetimes later,/ lay destroyed, beaten down,/ only the corpses of rebels/ ashes of dreams and blood stained streets./It has been written,/that those who have the youth/ have the future,/So come now children of the beast,/Be strong and shout at the devil."

The heavy metal groups themselves state that this is all in fun and that they are not into Satan worship. Whether this is true or not is not important. Young people feeling inadequate can have an instant sense of power from the music and identification closely with the lyrics. Heavy metal portrays the power and glory of evil. Adolescents with emotional and/or drug problems, which I treat every day, become further involved in delinquent behavior, violence, acts of cruelty and Satan worship. The glamorization of violence, sex, and drugs leads to further problems with directing young people's attitudes. Obviously, as a child psychiatrist, that is what I do, is try to help direct young people's attitudes and direct parents.

As Nikki Sixx of *Mötley Crüe* said in *Hit Parader*, "We like to live life to the fullest, and if that means driving your car into a wall at 70 miles per hour or doing three chicks at once, that's OK with us." In describing their form of music, "Yeah, apple pie, Chevrolet, tight jeans, *Mötley Crüe*, pizza, drugs and sex."

What is missing in today's teenagers identifying so strongly with heavy metal music? The music represents power, and the lyrics give purpose and meaning to those who have not been able to identify with the values they were raised with. Drugs and alcohol are often used while listening to heavy metal in order to feel the power more acutely and escape into the fantasies that are vividly portrayed on MTV. Escape alone may be harmless, but drug-induced altered states of consciousness combined with the message of hatred and violence in heavy metal is dangerous. There are problems in attitude, changes in thinking and new values develop.

Eighty-three percent of my patients have been listening to heavy metal for several hours per day, and over 50 percent know the words and write them down. And in fact, they do that in school, write down the words to the lyrics.

The drugs make the youngster suggestible to the message of the song. This is especially true with psychedelic mood-altering drugs, LSD, PCP and marijuana.

Heavy metal is presented to kids as a religion. The adolescents are vulnerable because their sense of identity has not been formed. Their sense of meaning and purpose in life is missing. They sense in themselves a need to rebel. The topics are sex, violence, and the power of evil. The emotional hunger in these young people is met in the form of music, chemical use, and promiscuous sexual behavior, the crazier, the better. The term "partying" refers to being under the influence of drugs and listening to the heavy metal music and lyrics. Drug dependent teenagers often party alone, soaking in the lyrics and allowing it to influence their attitudes. In heavy metal evil acts are glorified to new heights in concerts. Gunpowder is lit, people are hung and placed in coffins, demonic figures are produced, and property is destroyed. There are many stories about portrayal of evil acts on the stage, and the crowd goes wild.

One of the most pathological forms of evil is in the form of the cult killer or deranged person who believes it is OK to hurt others or to kill. The Son of Sam who killed eight people in New York was allegedly into *Black Sabbath's* music. Ricky Kasso, the teenager in Long Island who stabbed his friend, took out his eyes, and then hung himself, followed *Black Sabbath* and *Judas Priest*. That is in *Rolling Stone* in November 1984 where they interviewed the kids that were at the funeral.

Most recently, the individual identified by the newspapers as the Night Stalker has been said to be into hard drugs and the music of the heavy metal band *AC DC* .

This is not to say that the music made them into killers, but that in their insane, drug-crazed thinking, identification strongly with the lyrics of songs. I see the same process in my work with chemically dependent and hateful teenagers.

Every teenager who listens to heavy metal certainly does not become a killer. Young people who are seeking power over others through identification with the power of evil find a close identification. The lyrics become a philosophy of life. It becomes a religion. Young people in our treatment program recovering from drug problems, do, we ask them to give up heavy metal for at least a year so that they are not again overtaken by feelings of resentment, hate, and the urge to party. Partying, wich teens identify as a combination of drug use and hard rock music, is a strong stimulus to go back to that "Highway to Hell," which is an *AC DC* song.

Young teens who already think too much with their hormones and too little with their heads, succumb to heavy metal bombardment.

Thank you, Mr. Chairman.

The CHAIRMAN. Gentlemen thank you very much.

One 16-year-old music listener said to me – in fact, she is my daughter – you know, I really do not pay very much attention to the words. And my concern, said she, with labeling is that a label would simply underscore the fact that there are words here that really should be listened to, and that therefore, said she, labeling can make the situation worse, not better.

Do you think she has a good point or not?

Mr. STUESSY. I think she has a point there. Frequently that can in fact be the case. I think it is a matter of communicating to the record industry and related industries, whether it is through labeling, whether it is through ordinances such as are being considered today in San Antonio and other places, that we are not going to take this anymore. Do something. Clean up your act. Many of the problems Mr. Gortikove related just a few moments ago–that we cannot do this or that and if we print lyrics, then we might be guilty of pornography–there is a very simple answer. Get off that stuff; move on to something else. The industry itself creates the market for this.

The CHAIRMAN. Well, the industry could obviously stop making records that advocated this sort of behavior, but we are not talking about that today. All we are talking about is making information available to parents. The information that is available to parents is also available to children, and the question that was raised by my daughter was, well, does labeling not simply underscore the problem and call attention to it so that the kids are more likely to be paying attention to the words and, therefore, be influenced by the words more than otherwise?

Dr. KING. I do not feel that would happen. The young people who have serious drug problems are into the words. They specifically listen through the music for the lyrics because the lyrics give them the kinds of messages that they are looking for, rebellion, hate, violence, sex, the types of testimony that we have heard earlier. Those young people that do not listen for the lyrics pretty much are into just the beat of the music, and they know that some of the lyrics may be offensive, but they are not into it, so they do not listen for it. They just stay with the beat of the music.

The CHAIRMAN. You are saying the negative effect would not apply universally to everyone who heard the music, but it would apply to those people particularly on drugs who were susceptible to it.

Dr. KING. Yes, sir.

Mr. STUESSY. Nevertheless, even though an individual is not consciously absorbing the words, subconsciously they are being heard and registered.

The CHAIRMAN. Senator Gore.

Senator GORE. Thank you very much, Mr. Chairman.

I would like to first say it is nice to have a fellow Tennessean on the panel here. Dr. King practices in Memphis, and I am delighted to hear your testimony, and yours, Dr. Stuessy. In view of the lateness of the hour and the fact that we still have a panel to go, please forgive me if I just have a brief interchange with you.

If I could summarize the two presentations I would say both of you agree, based upon your experience, that there is a connection between messages received through this kind of material and behavior on the part of those who listen to it a lot or become really wrapped up in it. Is that a fair summary?

Dr. KING. Yes, that is a fair summary. That is what the patients tell me.

Mr. STUESSY. That is exactly right. We could fill the room with research studies to prove that.

Senator GORE. So there is not much disagreement about that fact?

Mr. STUESSY. Not really.

Senator GORE. Well, I may submit some additional questions in writing. It would not be onerous for you to resend in writing, if you would be willing to do so. We may just do it that way and save some time.

Thank you very much for your testimony.

Thank you, Mr. Chairman.

The CHAIRMAN. Thank you both very much.

Finally, we have a panel consisting of Mr. Eddie Fritts, president, National Association of Broadcasters; Mr. William Steding, executive vice president, Central Broadcasting Division, Bonneville International Corp.; Mr. Robert Sabatini, WRKC-FM, Wilkes-Barre, PA; and Mr.

Cerphe Colwell, Reston, VA.

Mr. Fritts, your name is first on the list. Why do you not proceed first.

STATEMENTS OF EDWARD O. FRITTS, PRESIDENT, NATIONAL ASSOCIATION OF BROADCASTERS; WILLIAM J. STEDING, EXECUTIVE VICE PRESIDENT, CENTRAL BROADCAST DIVISION, BONNEVILLE INTERNATIONAL CORP.; ROBERT J. SABATINI, JR., WRKC-FM, KING COLLEGE, WILKES-BARRE, PA; AND CERPHE COLWELL, RESTON, VA

Mr. FRITTS. Thank you, Mr. Chairman.

As you have mentioned, I represent the National Association of Broadcasters whose membership includes more than 4,500 radio stations and over 850 commercial television stations.

Of the 25,000 or so individual songs which are released each year, only a small number have lyrics which genuinely raise parental concern. As the principal trade association of the broadcasting industry, the main avenue of action for NAB when a problem such as the porn rock phenomenon arises is to generate industry awareness and sensitivity, and particularly the awareness of those at the top of our industry.

Thus, on May 13, 1985, I wrote executives of the more than 800 radio and television station group owners in the United States to alert them to the public concern that was developing over the issue of porn rock. Several articles have also been written on the subject for our weekly newsletter, which is sent to every NAB member.

The broadcasting industry response to my letter has been generally very favorable . In a number of cases senior executives wrote or told me in person that they had not been aware of the explicit nature of some of the music being played on their stations until they received my letter.

Some songs they found inappropriate for their audiences were removed from the play lists, and new songs are now being monitored more carefully. Additionally I believe the industry as a whole now has a higher level of sensitivity to this problem and to the general desirability of maintaining certain levels of good taste in programming.

A few weeks after I sent out my letter to the group owners, we discussed the porn rock problem at a meeting of the executive committee of the NAB board of directors. The conclusion which emerged was that we might be able to help our members respond by asking the record companies to supply copies of the lyrics when they make new records available to broadcasters. Thus, on May 31, 1985, I wrote to the chief executives of 45 record companies that together account in sales for about 85 percent of the Nation's recorded music, and I asked that all recordings made available to broadcasters in the future be accompanied by copies of the songs' lyrics.

Although there was a good deal of support for this proposal among broadcasters, the recording industry was not overwhelmed by the idea and subsequently rejected it.

Since we became involved in this issue, I and other members of the NAB staff have been in regular contact with Mrs. Tipper Gore and Mrs. Susan Baker and other leaders of the Parents Music Resource Center. Last week at the Radio Management and Programming Conference in Dallas, NAB sponsored a major session on this issue which I chaired. It featured presentations by Mrs. Gore and others from the PMRC, and by Stanley Gortikov, president of the RIAA, who graciously agreed to participate on the panel.

I view this panel as another step in our effort to make broadcasters understand the nature of the public concern about the issue so that they can formulate an appropriate response. The FCC expects each licensee to determine what the words or lyrics on a record are before the record is broadcast, and the FCC holds each broadcast licensee responsible for what it puts on the air. But even more importantly, broadcasters are held responsible in their local communities. If our listeners and our advertisers are not pleased with us, they will turn us off, the ultimate censor.

Each station must choose for itself how best to serve its own respective community, and not all listeners will like what every station in the marketplace has to offer. NAB will never attempt to intrude into any station's programming judgments. What we have endeavored to do is to balance the need for voluntary industry restraint with a strong sensitivity to first amendment concerns.

I think this effort has been successful. All in our industry now know that there is a problem which needs to be addressed and that they must make a conscious decision about how to respond to the concerns about porn rock as they go about serving their audiences in their respective communities.

Thank you, Mr. Chairman.

[The statement follows:]

STATEMENT OF EDWARD O. FRITTS, PRESIDENT, NATIONAL ASSOCIATION OF BROADCASTERS

Mr. Chairman, members of the Subcommittee, my name is Edward O. Fritts. I am president of the National Association of Broadcasters ("NAB"), an organization which represents more than 4500 radio stations, 850 television stations, and the major commercial broadcast networks. I appreciate the opportunity to join with you today to discuss the problem of what has come to be called "porn rock."

Before talking about what NAB has done to respond to this phenomenon, I think it is important to focus on the scope of the problem itself. More than 25,000 individual songs are released on record in the United States every year. Not all of these, of course, are rock music, and many recordings — much to the disapointment   of the artists and their record companies — rapidly go from release to obscurity. Nonetheless, it is important to remember that literally thousands of songs are competing form   public attention in the rock music marketplace each year.

Of this number, a small group have lyrics which are so sexually explicit or violent, or deal with the use of drugs and alcohol or with the occult in such a way as to raise some parental concern. Those parents who are concerned fear that the music at issue may have a detrimental impact on their children. Of this limited number of songs, only a very few ever receive any meaningful airplay.

I bring this information to the subcommittee's attention, Mr. Chairman, not to minimize the importance of the subject we are discussing today, but because — especially in several of the press reports in recent months — there has been some tendency to confuse the exceptions with the rule.

Now, what has NAB done to respond to this problem? As a trade association the main avenue of action open to us when a problem such as this arises is to generate industry awareness and sensitivity, and, particularly, the awareness of those at the top. Therefore, on May 13, 1985, I wrote executives of the more than 800 radio and television station group owners in the United States to alert them to the public concern that was developing over "porn rock." I included in that mailing the letter that the founders of what is now the Parents Music Resource Center had sent me on the subject, as well as a column from one of the major news magazines. That same week, I followed up on the mailing with a story in Highlights, our weekly newsletter for all NAB members, including a reprint of the text of the letter sent to the group owners.
The broadcasting industry response to my letter was generally very favorable.   Although a few broadcasts viewed even this informational mailing as a veiled attempt at censorship, many felt that it raised an issue deserving of immediate attention. Top management, even in relatively small station groups, must delegate most day-to-day decisions about what's on the air to program staff. In a number of cases, senior executives wrote or told me in person that they had not been aware of the explicit nature of some of the music being played on their stations until they received my letter. Some songs they found inappropriate for their audiences were removed from their playlists, and new releases are being monitored more carefully. Through the letter itself, and through numerous articles about the letter and the reaction to it which appeared in the trade press, I believe the industry now has a higher level of sensitivity to this problem, and to the general desirability of maintaining certain levels of good taste in programming. In many cases programming changes have been made, and that will continue. Several weeks after I sent out the letter to the group owners, we discussed the "porn rock" problem at a meeting of NAB's Executive Committee. That is the group of broadcasters elected by our Board of Directors to oversee the organization's day-to-day operations. The conclusion was that one way in which we might be able to help our members respond to the "porn rock" problem would be to ask the record companies to supply copies of the lyrics when

they make new records available to broadcasters.

Thus, on May 31, 1985, I wrote to the chief executives of 45 record companies that together account for the sales of over 90 percent of the nation's records, and asked that "all recordings made available to broadcasters in the future be accompanied by copies of the songs' lyrics." I explained that we were asking for this assistance not only to help the station program directors, but also to aid station owners and managers in going through the dozens of new releases, many of them recorded in a way that makes understanding the lyrics quite difficult.

Although there was a good deal of support for this proposal among broadcasters, our friends in the recording industry were not overwhelmed by the idea. Only a handful of responses were received, and they were generally negative in tone, although one very small company did send a copy of the lyrics it had supplied with a new singles release. Most recently, the Recording Industry Association of America has formally rejected the proposal on behalf of its members, arguing both that the record companies don't always have the right to reproduce lyrics for such purposes, and that it's the responsibility of every station to know what it broadcasts.

Since NAB got involved in this issue, I and other members of our staff have been in regular contact with Tipper Gore, Susan Baker and the other leaders of the Parents Music Resource Center. We have striven to understand their concerns, and to assist them in familiarizing themselves with the workings of our industry. Last week, at the Radio '85 Management and Programming Convention in Dallas, I chaired a panel session on "porn rock" which featured a lengthy presentation by Mrs. Gore. I am pleased that Stan Gortikov, the president of RIAA, also graciously agreed to participate on that panel. I view this panel as another step in our effort to make broadcasters aware of the public concern about this issue, so that they can formulate their own response.

The FCC expects each licensee to determine what the words or lyrics on a record are before the record is broadcast, and the FCC holds each broadcast licensee responsible for what it puts on the air. But even more importantly, broadcasters are held responsible by their local communities. We are there, every day. Indeed, every hour our communities vote on how well we are doing. If our listeners and our advertisers are not pleased with us, they will turn away, in the ultimate censure of our activity.

Each station must choose for itself how best to serve its community, and not all listeners will like what every station in the marketplace has to offer. That is part of the extraordinary diversity of our industry, and that is as it should be. NAB will never attempt to intrude into any station's programming judgments. That would be improper both legally and as a matter of policy. What we have endeavored to do is to balance the need for voluntary industry restraint with a strong sensitivity to First Amendment concerns. I think this effort has been successful. Everyone in our industry now knows that there is a problem to be addressed, and that they must make a conscious decision about how to respond to the concerns about "porn rock" as they go about serving their audiences.

I appreciate the consideration of the Subcommittee in permitting me to let you know of the action NAB has taken.

Thank you very much.

FRITTS LETTER TO BROADCAST STATION GROUPS

NATIONAL ASSOCIATION OF BROADCASTERS,
Washington, DC, May 13, 1985

DEAR   :

The lyrics of some recent rock records and the tone of the related music videos are fast becoming a matter of public debate. The subject has drawn national attention through articles in publications like Newsweek and USA Today and feature reports on TV programs like "Good Morning, America."
Many state that they are extremely troubled by the sexually explicit and violent language of some of today's songs. An example that has been cited is the song with words which say in part:

"I knew a girl named Nikki
I guess you could say she was a sex fiend
I met her in a hotel lobby
masturbating with a magazine."

The pre teen and teen audiences are heavy listeners, viewers and buyers of rock music. In some communities, like Washington. D.C., parents and other interested citizens are organizing to see what they can do about the music in question, which at least one writer has dubbed "porn rock."

I wanted you, as one of the leaders in the broadcasting industry, to be aware of this situation. For your information, I am enclosing the recent Newsweek column as well as a letter I received from a group of influential Washington area residents.

It is, of course, up to each broadcast licensee to make its own decisions as to the manner in which it carries out its programming responsibilities under the Communications Act.

Sincerely,

FRITTS LETTER TO RECORD COMPANIES

NATIONAL ASSOCIATION OF BROADCASTERS,
Washington, DC, May 31, 1985.

DEAR   :

I am writing you, as a leader in the recording industry, to ask your assistance in a matter of concern to many of us in broadcasting.

The sexually explicit and violent nature of some of today's songs raises difficult issues of selectivity for those broadcasters who program rock and other contemporary music. The sheer volume of new records (and videos) made available to broadcasters, as well as the recording techniques sometimes used, make it extremely difficult for broadcast owners, managers, and program   directors to be fully aware of the lyrics of all of the music their stations are being asked to air.

NAB has neither the ability nor the desire to place itself in any way in the role of censor of the music that broadcasters are presenting to the public. We do believe, however, that with your help we can play a constructive role by assisting broadcasters in making reasoned programming choices.

At its May meeting, NAB's Executive Committee asked that I write you to request that all recordings made available to broadcasters in the future be accompanied by copies of the songs' lyrics. It appears that providing this material to broadcasters would place very little burden on the recording industry, while greatly assisting the decisionmaking   of broadcast management and programming staffs.

I look forward to hearing from you on this proposal and learning your thoughts on the problem of selectivity that the broadcasting and recording industries confront.

Sincerely,

The CHAIRMAN. Thank you, Mr. Fritts.

Mr. Steding.

Mr. STEDING. First of all, I would like to take the opportunity to thank the Senate Commerce Committee for bringing together a panel of witnesses today for the purpose of analyzing carefully the…

[EDITOR'S NOTE: There seems to be a page missing from the website here because the next page takes you to the following letter]

FAITH CHRISTIAN FELLOWSHIP CHURCH,
Blue Ash, OH, September 13, 1985.

Senator BARRY GOLDWATER,
Senate Commerce Committee,
Washington, DC.

DEAR SENATOR GOLDWATER AND MEMBERS OF THE COMMERCE COMMITTEE:

I respectfully request that the sermon [The sermon was retained in the Committee files. entitled, Don't Let Them Do It, Daddy, containing important statistical data regarding pornography and audio pornography, as well as the attached petition, be added into the hearing record on behalf of the Faith Christian Fellowship Church. In addition, as a member of the Citizens Concerned For Community Values and as participants in the National Coalition Against Pornography, we ask that you stand against the dissemination of this material to the youth of our nation. Audio pornography has easy availability and we desire that a corrective and restraints be applied, so that the moral eyesight of our youth will not be gouged out. The corrupting influence of pornography in all of its forms degrades human life and results in deviant behavior.

Responsible leadership cannot neglect this important area of our national life.

Love, the highest form of sanity, demands that we protect our most important natural resource-the young people of this great country, who will represent our nation in future years. Therefore, it is our sincerer prayer that you wil repond [sic] and stop this hideous seduction.

Sincerely,

Rev. R. EDGAR BONNIWELL, M.Div., Th.M.

AMERICAN CIVIL LIBERTIES UNION,
Washington, DC, September 16, 1985.

Hon. JOHN C. DANFORTH,
Chairman, Senate Commerce, Science, and Transportation
Committee, Washington, DC

DEAR SENATOR DANFORTH:

I am writing to express the concern of the American Civil
Liberties Union regarding your upcoming September 19
hearing on proposals to label sound recordings with some
form of rating system or disclaimers to indicate their
contents.

In our view, it is inappropriate for a committee of the
United States Congress to serve as a set of official music
critics or to evaluate the content of lawfully produced and
distributed material. Virtually every newspaper, magazine,
and network talk show has chronicled the efforts of the
Parents Music Resource Center and other groups to "warn"
parents of lyrics which they claim present offensive ideas
about sex, violence, rejection of parental authority [,
substance abuse, or the occult. Although it is certainly
permissible for such private groups of parents, religious
leaders, or others to critique lyrics which they find
offensive for any reason, the effect of giving official
recognition to these positions through a Congressional
inquiry can cast a substantial chill over free expression.

The decision to hold hearings about song lyrics sends the
unmistakable signal to writers, producers, distributors, and
broadcasters of this form of music that their actions are
under scrutiny and that official intervention, in the form
of federal legislation, could descend on them from the wings.
These hearings seem designed not to warn parents about
content so much as to warn persons in the recording
industry then they must either "voluntarily" alter their
product or face new statutory or regulatory initiatives. The
threat of forthcoming censorship is palpable. This is
particularly true where the product is often marketed
through the regulated broadcasting industry. Any "label
warning" means that broadcasters will need to decide
whether to play "labelled" material and those who ignore
the labels will undoubtedly face pressue   at the time of
license renewal.

Recent witness lists indicate that a few songwriters will be present to address charges leveled   at rock music. It is certain that specific lyrics will be discussed as examples of what is "wrong" with rock music. The writers of all these lyrics will not be present to respond, even if that was their desire. Moreover, creative artists should not even be expected to explain or justify their work in an official forum such as a Congressional hearing.

The ACLU knows that many persons in the recording business feel great distress over Congressional activity in this arena. Although I realize that you are determined to hold these hearings, I wanted to voice out objections and ask that this letter be included in the record of the proceedings.

Sincerely,

BARRY W. LYNN,
Legislative Counsel.

GONZO Books

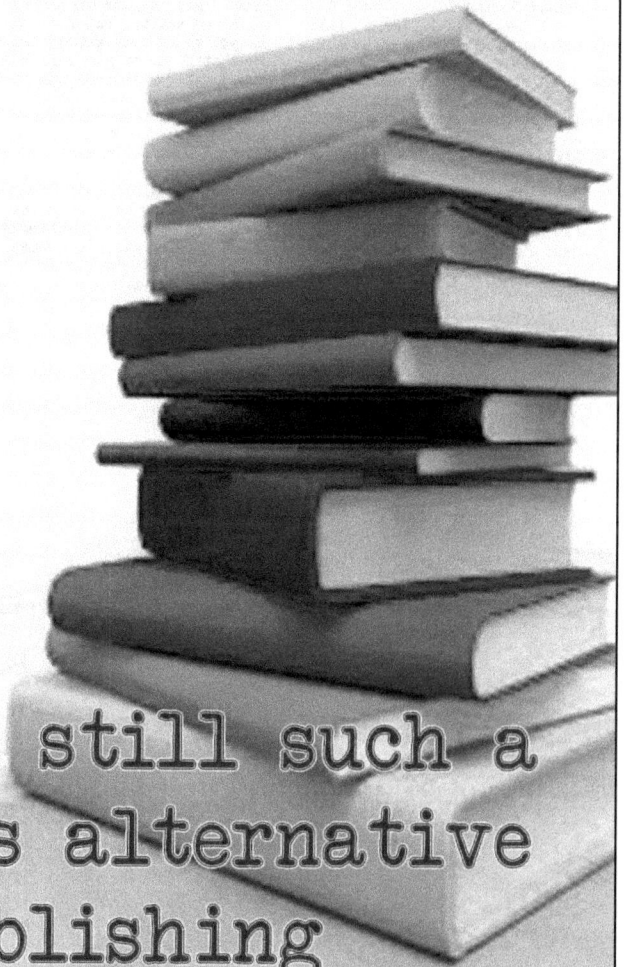

There is still such a thing as alternative Publishing

robert calvert
centigrade 232

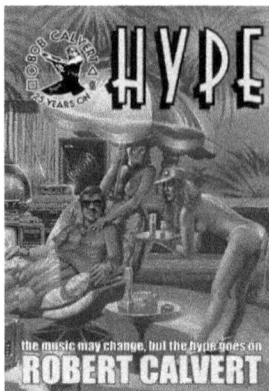

HYPE
the music may change, but the hype goes on
ROBERT CALVERT

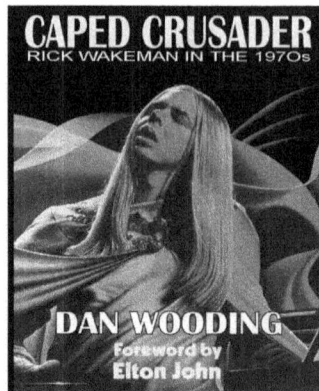

CAPED CRUSADER
RICK WAKEMAN IN THE 197Os

DAN WOODING
Foreword by
Elton John

Robert Newton Calvert: Born 9 March 1945, Died 14 August 1988 after suffering a heart attack. Contributed poetry, lyrics and vocals to legendary space rock band Hawkwind intermittently on five of their most critically acclaimed albums, including Space Ritual (1973), Quark, Strangeness & Charm (1977) and Hawklords (1978). He also recorded a number of solo albums in the mid 1970s. CENTIGRADE 232 was Robert Calvert's first collection of poems.

Hype   'And now, for all you speeding street smarties out there, the one you've all been waiting for, the one that'll pierce your laid back ears, decoke your sinuses, cut clean thru the schlock rock, MOR/crossover, techno flash mind mush. It's the new Number One with a bullet ... with a bullet ... It's Tom, Supernova, Mahler with a pan galactic biggie ...' And the Hype goes on. And on. Hype, an amphetamine hit of a story by Hawkwind collaborator Robert Calvert. Who's been there and made it back again. The debriefing session starts here.

Rick Wakeman is the world's most unusual rock star, a genius who has pushed back the barriers of electronic rock. He has had some of the world's top orchestras perform his music, has owned eight Rolls Royces at one time, and has broken all the rules of com posing and horrified his tutors at the Royal College of Music. Yet he has delighted his millions of fans. This frank book, authorised by Wakeman himself, tells the moving tale of his larger than life career.

"So many books, so little time."
Frank Zappa

THE NINE HENRYS
By Peter McAdam

TERRY DENE: BRITAIN'S FIRST ROCK & ROLL REBEL
DAN WOODING

King Squealer
MAURICE O'MAHONEY WITH DAN WOODING

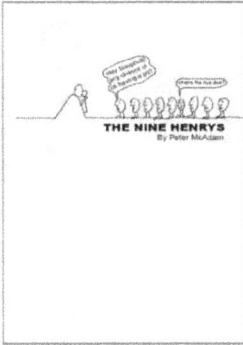

There are nine Henrys, pur ported to be the world's first cloned cartoon charac ter. They live in a strange lo fi domestic surrealist world peopled by talking rock buns and elephants on wobbly stilts.

They mooch around in their minimalist universe suffer ing from an existential crisis with some genetically modified humour thrown in.

Marty Wilde on Terry Dene: "Whatever happened to Terry becomes a great deal more comprehensible as you read of the callous way in which he was treated by people who should have known better many of whom, frankly, will never know better of the sad little shadows of the past who eased themselves into Terry's life, took everything they could get and, when it seemed that all was lost, quietly left him ... Dan Wood ing's book tells it all."

Rick Wakeman: "There have always been certain 'careers' that have fascinated the public, newspapers, and the media in general. Such include musicians, actors, sportsmen, police, and not surprisingly, the people who give the police their employ ment: The criminal. For the man in the street, all these careers have one thing in common: they are seemingly beyond both his reach and, in many cases, understanding and as such, his only associ ation can be through the media of newspapers or tele vision. The police, however, will always require the ser vices of the grass, the squealer, the snitch, (call him what you will), in order to assist in their investiga tions and arrests; and amaz ingly, this is the area that seldom gets written about."

"Outside of a dog, a book is man's best friend. Inside of a dog it's too dark to read."
Groucho Marx

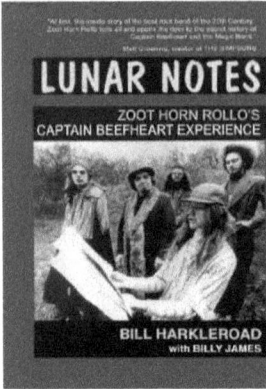

Bill Harkleroad joined Captain Beef heart's Magic Band at a time when they were changing from a straight ahead blues band into something completely dif ferent. Through the vision of Don Van Vliet (Captain Beefheart) they created a new form of music which many at the time considered atonal and difficult, but which over the years has continued to exert a powerful influence. Beefheart re christened Harkleroad as Zoot Horn Rollo, and they embarked on recording one of the classic rock albums of all time Trout Mask Replica - a work of unequalled daring and inventiveness.

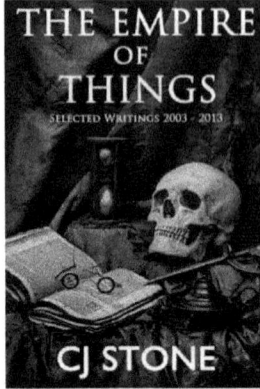

Politics, paganism and ... Vlad the Impaler. Selected stories from CJ Stone from 2003 to the present. Meet Ivor Coles, a British Tommy killed in action in September 1915, lost, and then found again. Visit Mothers Club in Erdington, the best psyche delic music club in the UK in the '60s. Celebrate Robin Hood's Day and find out what a huckle duckle is. Travel to Stonehenge at the Summer Solstice and carouse with the hippies. Find out what a Ranter is, and why CJ Stone thinks that he's one. Take LSD with Dr Lilly, the psychedelic scientist. Meet a headless soldier or the ghost of Elvis Presley in Gabalfa, Cardiff. Journey to Whitstable, to New York, to Malta and to Transylvania, and to many other places, real and imagined, polit ical and spiritual, transcendent and mundane. As The Independent says, Chris is "The best guide to the underground since Charon ferried dead souls across the Styx."

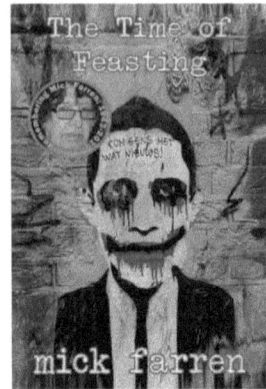

This is is the first in the highly acclaimed vampire novels of the late Mick Farren. Victor Renquist, a surprisingly urbane and likable leader of a colony of vampires which has existed for centuries in New York is faced with both admin istrative and emotional prob lems. And when you are a vampire, administration is not a thing which one takes lightly.

"The person, be it gentleman or lady, who has not pleasure in a good novel, must be intolerably stupid."

Jane Austen

www.ingramcontent.com/pod-product-compliance
Lightning Source LLC
Chambersburg PA
CBHW070845300326
41935CB00039B/1484